No more recent ed. is in print 1/96.

AF814857

1992
ELECTRIC VEHICLE DIRECTORY

by

Philip Terpstra

SONOMA COUNTY LIBRARY
1000 06 141495 0 4

Terpstra, Philip.
Electric vehicle
directory : 1992 /
1991.

1000061414950 4
CENT

SONOMA COUNTY LIBRARY
OFFICIAL
DISCARD

Printed in the U.S.A. on recycled paper

ELECTRIC VEHICLE DIRECTORY

Copyright © 1991
by Philip Terpstra

No part of this book may be reproduced in any form, including mechanical, photocopying, recording, electronic, or any other means, without prior written permission from the author. Brief passages may be quoted without permission for purposes of review or in writing to legislators. No liability is assumed with respect to the use of information in this book.

Many of the photos in this book were provided by the sellers of the electric cars. I wish to thank them. No copyright is claimed by the author for such material, but it may be protected by other copyrights.

Front cover photo: 4E Corporation's five–place EXAR–1
(courtesy of 4E Corporation)

Back cover photo: Tropical rainforest, Belize, C. America
(photo by Linda Terpstra)

For advertising, bulk purchases, or other information contact:

SPIRIT PUBLICATIONS
P.O. Box 23417
Tucson, Arizona 85734
U.S.A.

SPIRIT

ABOUT THE PAPER USED IN THIS BOOK

I seek to make this directory of relatively benign technology available in a form that will itself make the least negative impact on the natural environment.

The text of this book is printed on recycled white paper. Using recycled paper obviously saves trees. Every one thousand copies of this book printed on paper made from waste rather than virgin pulp saves about three trees. The importance of trees in maintaining a healthy environment can hardly be overemphasized.

Recycled paper also has other environmental benefits. In most paper mills chlorine is used to remove lignin from the wood pulp used to make the paper. Lignin is an organic compound that binds together the cellulose fibers in trees and other woody plants. Paper that still contains lignin quickly yellows when exposed to sunlight. The chlorine and other chemicals used to delignify the wood may combine with each other and with natural substances in the wood to form dioxin. Dioxin is a highly toxic group of compounds. Some dioxins have been used in chemical warfare (e.g., Agent Orange). By using paper that has already gone through the delignification process, recycling greatly reduces the amount of dioxin produced in the paper making process. Chlorine is also often used to bleach the paper; this produces even more dioxin. Recycled paper uses 75 percent less chlorine in the bleaching stage. (Some paper mills use hydrogen peroxide or other chemicals to bleach paper; this is generally kinder to the environment than the use of chlorine.)

Though some paper mills have been notorious polluters, it should be noted here that the paper industry produces less than 3 percent of the dioxin that is released into the environment. Steel and other metal production, sewage sludge from municipal water treatment facilities, incineration of solid waste, and emissions from vehicles powered by internal combustion engines are the primary sources of dioxin. Still, there is room for more improvement in the papermaking process.

White recycled paper is still more expensive than paper made from virgin pulp. Strange as it seems, it is still cheaper to cut down trees, haul them to roads, take them to mills, clean them, and turn them into paper, than to turn waste paper back into usable paper. Subsidies paid for virgin paper are partly to blame for this. Also, not enough money has been spent on R & D or tooling for the recycling process. As the demand for this paper increases and the recycling techniques improve, prices will undoubtedly come down.

ABOUT THE INK USED IN THIS BOOK

The text and cover of this book are printed with soybean-oil-based ink. The production and use of agricultural-based inks is a relatively recent development. These inks became available in 1989 and are no more expensive than conventional inks. In most inks petroleum products make up about 60 percent of the total ink volume. In the printing process such petrochemicals give off large amounts of toxic volatile organic compounds. Using refined soybean/corn oil instead of petrochemicals for the ink's vehicle and binder is much better for the environment. The benefits include:

- Vegetable-oil-based inks reduce the amount of toxic VOCs given off in the printing process by 80 percent or more.

- Corn and soybeans are renewable natural resources.

- By using agricultural-based inks, we help support the farming community. Farmers are paid to provide a needed product, rather than being paid to let their land lie idle.

- If all the printing companies in the U.S.A. used soy or corn inks rather than petroleum inks, this country's oil imports could be reduced by 5 to 6 percent, which is about the same amount of oil imported from Iraq in 1989.

- The processing of vegetable oils is cleaner than the refining of petroleum oil. This, too, reduces the amount of pollutants released into the environment.

- In a garbage dump (let's call it what it is, rather than using the euphemism "landfill") vegetable oils are biodegradable; petroleum oils are not. But please recycle this book rather than throwing it away.

- Vegetable-oil inks are easier to clean up than petroleum based inks, allowing the use of non-toxic cleansing solutions on printing equipment.

- These inks are safer for the producers, printers, and readers.

ELECTRIC VEHICLE DIRECTORY

CONTENTS

PREFACE

This directory is intended for use by individuals interested in building or buying an EV, as well as by designers and manufacturers who need quick access to business information. Many manufacturers listed in the back of the Directory will not sell their products retail, though they may provide a list of local dealers. If you are interested in purchasing items retail, please note whether the company listed is a manufacturer or a supplier, before you invest time and postage. Also, it is generally a good idea to include a SASE (self-addressed, stamped envelope) when requesting information. Many suppliers and conversion companies are small businesses on tight budgets run by one or two people. Some companies, including Spirit Publications, remain nonprofit groups, though that is not the intention. Often the owners work or attend school full or part time in addition to operating their own businesses. Their motivation is not primarily profit, but to offer environmentally safer alternatives to what is more commonly available. If they are inundated with requests they simply may not have the resources to respond to everyone. Your courtesy is appreciated.

The present momentum of the EV industry is mainly the result of the efforts of these small businesses working very hard to develop and promote this gentler technology. The large corporate automakers, which have vast resources and political and economic connections, could have made EVs available long ago. But it's the small businesses struggling along that have helped raise public awareness to such a point that the big automakers are now getting into the act. Hopefully the small companies won't be tossed aside by political or economic pressures when EVs become the main form of road transportation.

I have expended much effort to ensure the accuracy and completeness of this Directory, but there are undoubtedly some errors and omissions. In preparing for this fourth edition we sent out a few hundred questionnaires; many were not returned to us. Many follow-up phone calls were also made, but I still don't know the status of some enterprises. A few listings were dropped, as it's frustrating for readers to attempt to contact a company, only to find that they are out of business. Reader feedback is appreciated regarding companies that are not listed but should be.

The primary purpose of this publication is to provide readers with up-to-date information on EVs and related products that are available today, years ahead of Detroit or Japan. Some information is given pertaining to ongoing research and products that are not as yet available, as this is of interest to some readers for a point of comparison. But that is not the main focus of the book. Almost all large auto manufacturers in the world are developing or experimenting with EVs. They finally realize that drivers will be demanding more environmentally benign forms of personal transportation. You won't find the latest news about Toyota or Ford EV projects here. The best source for that would be an EV newsletter.

Dimensional specifications are given in metric (the international standard) and in English measurements. Only two countries in the world still *officially* use the archaic English system, but it is in common use by many people. The only difficulty in using metric alone is the continuing desire of some people to convert the measurements into English figures. For those who think, measure, and make comparisons in metric, there is no difficulty. It is a far easier and more logical system of measurement. Some tools, such as wrenches and sockets, would need to be changed over for metric use, but the majority of tools are usable with any system of measurement. It's unfortunate that new generations are always being burdened with an archaic and clumsy measuring system.

Please keep in mind that all prices and specifications given are subject to change without notice and should be used as a general guide only. Though prices often go up, on some items they come down as demand increases and manufacturing methods improve.

INTRODUCTION

The selection of battery-powered road vehicles is expanding. The general public still seems to think of electric cars as slow-moving, impractical curiosities. This myth is being proved false at many EV races in the U.S.A., Australia, Switzerland, and other countries.

The U.S.A. still "leads" the world in both the per-capita and total number of passenger cars. Somewhere around 140 million personal vehicles are in regular use in this country. The environmental effects are devastating. Aside from the obvious and deadly air-pollution problem, the use and improper disposal of antifreeze, lubricating oil, and various additives produce toxic effects on the natural environment.

ALTERNATIVE FUELS

Most alternative fuels currently available offer little hope, though further research in this area is definitely worthwhile. Propane is a relatively clean-burning fuel, but it is not available in large enough quantities to allow its use in cars on a massive scale. Methanol and natural gas are also rather clean-burning fuels, but they still pollute and do nothing to eliminate the noise, requirement for antifreeze, and other problems associated with inefficient two- or four-stroke cycle internal-combustion engines (ICEs).

Hydrogen is a promising fuel. It is very clean-burning, and the solution to the storage difficulties of this fuel is close at hand. Hydrogen has the potential to be used in a great variety of applications, including transport category aircraft, for which electric propulsion is not yet feasible with present battery technology.

But using hydrogen to fuel vehicles equipped with ICEs wouldn't be the best use of this substance. Four-stroke cycle engines have a peak efficiency of about 25 percent in converting the chemical energy in fuel into mechanical energy to move a vehicle. They have hundreds of moving parts that wear out and need replacement (requiring, in turn, energy-consuming and toxic manufacturing processes).

A more promising application of hydrogen as a fuel for road vehicles is in the use of fuel-cells. In such a system the hydrogen produces the electricity that powers an EV. This is especially promising for buses and other large vehicles.

EVs OFFER THE MOST HOPE

Electric road vehicles are the most promising and practical solution to the present problems associated with ICE-powered cars. EVs produce no exhaust, and even those recharged from pollution-producing electric power plants still allow a significant reduction in total air pollution. This is because electric utilities are far more efficient at producing power than are most car engines, and EVs do not waste energy while stopped in traffic. According to the California Air Resources Board (CARB), an EV produces only one-tenth of the pollution emitted by an ICE car, even when recharged from a grid source that burns fossil fuels.

Petroleum prices may rise and fall, but eventually this nonrenewable resource is going to be depleted. And aside from the fuel availability issue, the environmental problems associated with its use do not go away.

There's still a big mess in the Persian Gulf, including the environmental havoc intentionally wrought by Saddam Hussein in lighting the oil fires. Both Iraq's and the U.S.A.'s military actions in the area were motivated primarily by an interest in petroleum. It would be good to wipe out the market for this stuff. In the war against ivory poachers, leaders finally realized they had to stop the sale of ivory products in order to protect elephants. Merely going after poachers doesn't work well. So it is with oil. There are many politicians and big business interests that are working hard to drill for new oil in remote natural areas in Alaska, Ecuador, and many other parts of the world. Various groups are trying to stop that action directly. But we also need to stop the problem at the source. Many will continue seeking ways to damage the earth for petroleum as long as a market for it exists.

Although EVs were becoming popular in the late 1970s and early '80s, that whole momentum nearly dissolved with the anti-environmental policies of the Reagan administration. It would be good if that eight-year setback were over, but the Bush administration is no better. In his election campaign, Bush claimed that he would be the "environmental president". Apparently that was one of many empty promises. Both Reagan and Bush make Jimmy Carter look great by comparison, and not only concerning environmental issues. Jimmy, we're sorry that you didn't make it in 1980. Many things would be much better now if you had. Undoubtedly the moneylenders who control the flow of politics wanted us to have the different kind of leadership they subsequently gave us.

Because so little money has been spent on EV development compared to the billions of dollars spent on R & D for ICE vehicles, there is little wonder that there are still some problems with EVs. Certainly there will be teething pains for any new (or newly revised) industry; but as more and more people buy EVs, more money will be available for further R & D. That, and user feedback, will undoubtedly improve the vehicles.

Ten years ago those who were willing and financially able to replace their dinosaur-consuming ICE cars with EVs paid a higher price in money and lack of convenience, while the decreased pollution (though immeasurably small) was shared by everyone in the area. Tax incentives should be made available so that considerate and caring individuals can have some financial benefit for being kind to the environment. In some places the policies are the opposite of what they should be. Oregon, for example, charges much greater licensing fees for electric cars than for standard vehicles. Allegedly this is to make up for the fact that EV owners don't pay the road taxes charged in gasoline sales. The newly formed Oregon electric vehicle association is planning to address this backwards policy.

THE COST OF PETROLEUM

Well-informed people know that the true cost of gasoline is not measured at the pump. The military expenditures to protect oil sources and other tax subsidies must also be considered. The health threats (including cancer) and other problems involved with petroleum also add tremendously to the real cost. But if only one or two car owners per thousand switch to electric power, they still have to deal with the side-effects of gasoline. That's one reason that the move to environmentally safer products is so slow — the immediate cost is still higher for the individual, but he gains very little if others don't join. By raising the gasoline taxes so that the pump price is $2 or 3 per gallon (as it is in much of the world), there would be an economic disincentive to stay addicted to petroleum. This is one reason that much of western Europe is way ahead of the U.S.A. on per-capita use of bicycles and all sorts of low-energy-use appliances.

PRESENT DRAWBACKS OF EVs

There are, of course, some difficulties with EVs at present. Among these are higher purchase prices, limited daily range, long recharge times, and the need for auxiliary heaters. The price of a ready-to-drive new (or newly converted) four-wheeled electric car is about the same as that of a small luxury car. At present there are almost no used EVs available. It's impossible for the average janitor or waitress to pay $25,000 for a new EV, but he or she could probably buy a used dinosuar-consuming car for $1,000 without too much trouble. We're not yet on the threshold of replacing all ICE cars with EVs. Fortunately, there are some light-weight three-wheelers to choose from. One or more of these may soon be available for under $15,000. That's a good start. Another promising development is the EXAR-1. Already mentioned in last year's Directory, this car may be going into production soon. One of the company's goals is to offer the EXAR-1 for the excellent price of $12,000 — for a turn-key vehicle designed from the start to be powered by electricity — if economic realities allow it.

The daily range of most EVs is between 50 and 100 miles. This presents no problem for most commuters, but it is a drawback for some other operations The U.S. Postal Service had a fleet of about 500 electric postal trucks about twelve years ago. These vehicles were equipped with expensive deep-cycle lead-acid batteries. The trucks were used on a daily basis, loaded down with mail, and driven all day (or until the batteries ran down). Many such trucks could not finish their rounds and had to be towed in. With the batteries so deeply discharged every day, they would no longer hold a full charge, and had to be replaced much sooner than anticipated. The few such EVs used by the Post Office in northern climates had to be equipped with fuel-oil heaters; these heaters used as much fuel as a regular truck needed for all its power, so there was no gain financially or environmentally. Understandably, the Postal Service found these vehicles unacceptable for their purposes. It's unfortunate that EVs were pressed into such rigorous service so early in their evolutionary history.

But most commuters don't have these requirements. Though still not great, better battery technology is commercially available today, and more promising alternatives are now being developed. Lightweight and efficient heat pumps (such as that used in the GM Impact) may be a good solution to the heating and cooling requirements of the passenger compartments.

BETTER BATTERIES

Presently available lead-acid batteries must be replaced every 20,000 to 30,000 miles. In a small car, this can cost from $500 to $1,500, depending on the type and quantity of the batteries. Some people emphasize this fact to "prove" that EVs are financially impractical. Of course, they ignore the fact that ICE-powered cars require oil and filter changes, tune-ups, replacement of spark plugs, etc., etc. Add up all those costs incurred for the same number of miles traveled and you will find that battery replacement doesn't look so bad. Battery development continues, with research being done to improve Nickel-Zinc, Nickel-Iron, Lithium, Aluminum-Air, and Zinc-Air batteries.

Lead-acid batteries, the mainstay of present EVs, have had a good history of recycling. When customers buy lead-acid EV or SLI batteries, they bring in their old units as cores. This excellent system has functioned well for many years and should easily be adaptable to other battery types. This is an especially important consideration with batteries that use heavy metals, in order to keep them out of garbage dumps

This Honda CRX conversion is equipped with Dreisbach ElectroMotive's experimental Zinc-Air batteries and has a considerable driving range.

or other places where they could contaminate ground water or streams.

In the first annual SERA 500 electric car race in Phoenix in April of 1991, Dreisbach ElectroMotive, Inc., had a Honda CRX converted into an EV and powered by their experimental Zinc-Air batteries. This vehicle won the competition. Later in the year, on August 29, it broke the distance record for continuous travel by a battery-powered car. Traveling at between 30 and 40 mph, the electric CRX covered 251 miles without recharging.

Most Japanese automakers are working on EV prototypes. Nissan, that nation's second-largest (after Toyota) auto manufacturer is developing some new lead-acid batteries that dissipate heat more rapidly and can be recharged in 15 minutes. That's hardly any longer than it takes to refill a gasoline tank. These batteries are said to weigh only half as much as conventional batteries. Installed in their FEV (Future Electric Vehicle), they will propel the car to 130 kph (81 mph). At a more moderate speed of 72 kph (45 mph), the car has a range of 160 kilometers (100 miles).

RENEWABLE ENERGY SOURCES

Along with electric vehicles, we need alternate sources to generate electricity. Electric utilities readily admit that large-scale use of EVs would increase their profits. Hopefully this will also encourage them to seek alternative ways of generating electricity. Recharging EVs with grid electricity from fossil-fueled utilities would still result in a substantial improvement in air quality, for reasons mentioned earlier. But still, this would shift the main pollution problem from vehicles to electric power stations. This would keep city air cleaner but create a greater pollution in the outlying areas. And, of course, these utilities are burning up nonrenewable forms of fuel, much of it coming from unstable political sources. Long-wall coal mining has also proven to be destructive to farms and other land under which the coal is found.

Electricity produced from solar power probably has the most promise. Photovoltaics have been in use on a small scale for about three decades, and they require no maintenance. Their efficiency is slowly improving, and some excellent price-reduction breakthroughs appear close.

Solar-thermal setups have been more effective for large-scale use. About 95 percent of electricity produced commercially from solar power comes from this type of system. The Luz company developed several such facilities that are currently operating in southern California. This system uses mirrors to focus the sun's rays to boil water; the resulting steam spins turbines to produce electricity. Unfortunately, the utilities that burn fossil fuels are the ones that get huge government subsidies, making it hard for the environmentally sound operations to compete.

Meanwhile, individuals can purchase their own photovoltaic solar panels for recharging their EVs. This is especially useful in rural areas where grid electricity, if available at all, is quite expensive. Where we live, west of Tucson, grid electricity costs 12 cents per kilowatt hour. A 2,500-pound EV recharged from such a power source would require about 7.7 cents per mile in electricity use — equivalent to only 13 miles per gallon at $1.00 per gallon of gasoline. A very small system with PV panels and a charger could easily be set up (for a price!) in a small house lot. For EVs that are driven only a few times a week and for short distances, PV panels mounted on the roof of the vehicle could provide all of the electricity needed, if a constant trickle charge system was used. At least one person in Phoenix has his small Ford set up this way. With the car parked in the sun at work or at home, the batteries are always receiving a small charge. He can justifiably feel good about his driving, as all of his fuel is free (after the initial investment, of course), renewable, and nonpolluting. Right now there are about 43 million operational cars that are driven less than 20 miles per day. A large percentage of these car owners could probably benefit from such a PV system.

But for those who do need to drive more and/or do not live in areas with so much sunshine, PVs mounted on the vehicle may not be practical at all. Stationary PV arrays, such as could be set up on a house rooftop, can allow a greater surface area to be exposed to the sun's rays. Large companies with huge parking lots could set up PV charging systems with metered outlets, so their employees or customers can charge up their EVs.

An additional incentive to encourage the use of renewable energy is to avoid the push by some groups for nuclear plants. Pronounced "noo-kyoo-ler" by many, nuclear energy has proven to be unsafe in many ways. Aside from the obvious potential for more tragic in-plant accidents, no one has ever come up with a suitable solution for the disposal of spent but still radioactive fuel. The proposal, "Let's just ship it to Nevada" understandably is not met with rejoicing by residents of that state. The problem can be avoided by not using nuclear power.

LEGISLATION

Southern California, with some serious air-pollution problems, has probably been the single biggest push to recent EV development. Recently the California Air Resources Board mandated that by 1998, two percent of a car manufacturer's sales in that state must be zero-emission vehicles (ZEVs). Currently, only EVs qualify as ZEVs. This requirement rises to 10 percent (or about 200,000 cars) for the year 2003.

Other states are following California's lead and are considering legislation regarding exhaust-emission levels and alternative fuels. The federal Clean Air Act calls for higher-mileage cars and reduced emissions but of course does nothing about the overpopulation problem, which tends to negate these small improvements. Besides, as others have noted, people who switch to high-mileage vehicles tend to drive them more, thus using up just as much fuel.

ASSOCIATIONS AND EVENTS

There are a number of electric-vehicle associations around the world. Many of these have been in existence for over ten years. They have helped spread general awareness of EVs as well as technical knowledge about them. Members help one another in building EVs or converting ICE cars to electric power. In recent years some such organizations have become increasingly involved with efforts to change legislation in favor of EVs.

Most of these groups are autonomous organizations, each of which is located in just one metropolitan area. As yet there is no very large EV organization with a great number of members and substantial political influence. This may be coming, though. The Electric Auto Association, one of the oldest EV groups, is also the largest. They have about six chapters in California and at least that many in the rest of the U.S.A.

Another positive step is a growing number of electric-vehicle events in several places around the world. The Swiss Tour de Sol has been around for about five years and promotes solar-car races. Australia has several groups that organize similar events there. Others are based in Arizona, California, and Massachusetts. These racing events promote competition and effective testing of EVs, as well as an opportunity for people in the industry to get together and share knowledge and ideas. And, of course, a very important aspect of these events is increasing public awareness of EVs. Although the political situation in the U.S.A. regarding the environment is no better now than it was during the infamous Reagan years, these various groups are forging ahead to prove that EVs are practical now, and to provide means for improving the technology.

ADDITIONAL CONSIDERATIONS

Another issue in the EV industry has been the need for an attractive magazine on the subject that bookstores and supermarkets would be willing to stock. Magazine racks everywhere are full of periodicals on fuel-guzzling noisy hot-rods and luxury cars. But there has been nothing on EVs. The individuals or small groups that would like to produce such a publication do not have enough financial capital to do it. However, long-time EV user and author Michael Hackleman started a promising publication last year. Entitled *Alternative*

Transportation News, it deals in large measure with EVs but also covers other relatively benign transportation forms. It is good to keep the options open. Hopefully this and other new publications will be carried on newsstands, where they can be seen by the general public.

I hope this directory will also be instrumental in raising public awareness of EVs. The big auto manufacturers have always been interested in profits, not the environment. When those who can afford to buy new cars realize that electric vehicles are practical now, I hope they will be concerned and well-enough informed to make a green choice.

ADVANTAGES OF EVs

1. **Less Air Pollution.** According to the California Air Resources Board, EVs produce only one-tenth of the pollutants emitted by ICE-powered cars, even after figuring in the emissions from fossil-fuel burning power plants used to recharge the cars. EVs recharged from solar, wind, or other nonpolluting energy sources produce no air pollution at all. This reduced pollution means a great slowing of the degradation of statues, priceless old stained glass, and buildings in city centers.

2. **Quiet Operation.** There is no noisy exhaust, valve train clatter, or knocking.

3. **Reduced Dependency on Foreign Oil.** This can reduce a country's trade deficit and a country's desire to go to war over oil. It also slows the flow of money to some despotic tyrants in the Middle East.

4. **Reduced Maintenance.** EVs don't need tune-ups, spark-plug changes, oil changes, oil filters, fuel filters, antifreeze, radiator flushes, fuel or water pumps, or exhaust system repairs. (Have you checked your muffler bearings lately?)

5. **Health Improvements.** Petrochemicals, their fumes, and exhaust from their burning have known carcinogenic effects.

6. **Driving Safety.** Not needing 6 quarts of lubricating oil (what little oil is needed is not contaminated by combustion processes), EVs will not leak this slippery commodity onto road surfaces. Gasoline is a highly flammable substance that greatly increases the danger in automobile accidents. EVs do not use gasoline.

7. **Reliability.** Belt and hose failure are common causes of highway breakdowns of standard cars. Add to this the incredible complexity of a four-stroke cycle reciprocating engine and their fuel and ignition systems, and it's a wonder cars don't break down more often. Electric motors used in EVs have only one main moving part. Controllers are solid state. EVs have very little to break down. The only worry this causes is for some auto makers, as they won't be able to make nearly as much money on spare parts. That's their problem.

8. **Lower "Fuel" Costs.** Although not true in all areas, it is certainly true in much of southern California, with higher gasoline prices and very low electricity rates. Millions of drivers could benefit from this advantage.

9. **Immense Reduction In Oil Spills.** Widespread replacement (not augmentation) of ICE cars with EVs would reduce oceanic oil spills and the horrendous amount of crude and refined fuel that leaks into the ground and water from leaky storage tanks. These environmental advantages will probably be partially offset by number 4 on the next page.

DRAWBACKS OF EVs WITH PRESENT TECHNOLOGY

1. **Need for auxiliary heater and defroster.** High–efficiency heat–pumps will solve much of this difficulty.

2. **Higher initial cost than for ICE car.** This is definitely true for most EVs at present. But as the demand and subsequent manufacturing capabilities increase, the per unit cost can come down. As EVs have much less mechanical complexity that ICE cars, they will very likely become less expensive than comparably equipped (aesthetics, luxury, etc.) ICE cars.

3. **Short driving range.** With very short recharge–time batteries on the way, this becomes almost a non–argument. As the market for EVs grows, battery manufacturers will have more incentive to do further R & D and more capital with which to do it. Many convenience stores, doughnut shops, present fuel stations, etc., could be equipped with metered electricity outlets for fast EV recharging. This infrastructure will take time to expand, but its growth will likely be rapid as business owners recognize the market potential.

4. **Increased mining for lead and/or other materials for batteries.** Here again, good recycling of battery material will help reduce this requirement. Unlike batteries, gasoline is not recycled. It's burned up, and we have to keep going back into the ground for more.

How do nations rate on the per-capita use of automobiles? A great number of vehicles per person results in congested traffic and a high degree of wasted resources. It is important to find alternative ways of achieving personal freedom and mobility, rather than to assume that each individual should own a car. many "freeways" in Los Angeles, San Francisco, Phoenix, and other large cities, become parking lots many hours each day, as traffic comes to a stop. That is not freedom but slavery. Mass transit with convenient schedules would be one good alternative.

Calculated from information in the 1991 edition of *The World Almanac and Book of Facts,* here are some interesting comparisons. The countries below are ranked according to per-capita use. Number one has the most cars per person - I wouldn't equate that with being best.

Rank	No. of cars per person	No. of people per car	Total no. of cars
1. U.S.A.	.56	1.88	139,000,000
2. Australia	.52	1.91	8,700,000
3. Iceland	.48	2.07	121,000
4. West Germany*	.47	2.12	28,800,000
5. Luxembourg	.455	2.2	168,000
6. Canada	.42	2.39	11,100,000
7. Italy	.40	2.47	23,300,000
8. France	.39	2.57	21,900,000
9. New Zealand	.38	2.6	1,300,000
? C. African Republic	.00035	2,879.0	1,000

* Figures for reunited Germany not available.

CONVERT OR BUILD FOR PURPOSE?

Since the early 1970s there has been some debate as to the best method for producing electric cars. Two basic methods exist — either convert an existing car to electric propulsion, or build a car that is designed from the beginning to be an EV. Many types from each school of thought have already been built are are operating, so obviously both types can function. The question remains as to which system is the most efficient.

Proponents of the conversion method point out that there are many old ICE cars lying around that are in good shape except for the engine. The engine and associated equipment can be removed and an electric motor, controller, batteries, etc., can be installed. This offers some economy, since the whole vehicle is already there, and with much depreciation having already taken place, the purchase price is quite low. Reusing a product is an important goal.

Presently, the demand for EVs is *much* greater than the supply. Hopefully, many present automotive shops will devote part of their labor and facilities to converting cars to electric power. There is definitely a big market for this. Customers could drop off their fossil-fuel burning cars, come back a week or two later, and drive away with the same car, no longer producing air pollution. Come on, entrepreneurs, how about setting up the first (or tenth?) such facility in your town?

Another advantage of the conversion method is that the ride comfort and aesthetics to which a car owner may be accustomed remain essentially unchanged. A large number of people who might want to purchase an EV don't want to stand out from the crowd visibly. By buying a converted car, they can move along rather inconspicuously while driving a basically nonpolluting vehicle.

Other people *do* want to own something different. They want to feel distinctive while driving a car that is much kinder to the environment. But a common complaint about

The Earth Options/Solar Electric Corporation in Santa Rosa, California is one of a growing number of facilities that converts standard cars to electric power.

EVs in the late 1970s and early '80s is that many of them looked like a cross between a golf cart and a telephone booth. It is certainly puzzling that some EV designers created such ugly machines. Several new designs, thankfully, don't have this problem. The Doran ZEV (page 28) is distinctive and attractive. Beauty is in the eye of the beholder, and homebuilt cars can be slightly modified to suit individual taste. Hopefully more companies will build EVs that take appearance into consideration. Though aesthetics shouldn't be the number one factor affecting a purchase, it is important to customers, and EV designers should be sensitive to that fact.

Purpose-built EVs probably have more advantages than conversions. In designing an EV from the ground up, the engineer(s) has the opportunity to integrate the various components so that they work most efficiently together. [From this description, the term "ground-up design" originated as an alternate label for "purpose-built." But "ground-up" sounds a little like hamburger.] In most (if not all) conversions, the resulting EV has a greater empty weight than it did as an ICE vehicle. It may have a higher center of gravity and/or other weight distribution differences that could affect handling. Purpose-built EVs can be both smaller *and* lighter than converted cars of the same capacity. Elroy Engineering of Australia, Clean Air Transport of Sweden, and the 4E Corporation of the U.S.A., are among those who have built successful EV prototypes of this kind.

It is a sad fact that many cars drag around 2,000 kilograms of vehicle weight just to transport a sole 80 kilogram occupant. Very few corporations in the U.S.A. build lightweight two place cars (They are more common in Europe). So there is little to choose from for converting to electric power if one desires to have a very light and small vehicle. By mounting the motors in the wheels or other optimum location, the purpose-built EV can have an additional advantage over a conversion, which requires working with what's already there.

Over the years, many small companies in the U.S.A. and Europe offered new EVs that were actually conversions of ICE cars. That is, the conversion company would buy a new production vehicle without the engine and associated drive train components from the manufacturer. But the price of this basic car (to the "middle" company) was not reduced nearly as much as the value of the missing items. So, by the time the conversion company had added the motor, batteries, controller, etc., they ended up with a heavier and much more expensive vehicle. Understandably, potential customers were unimpressed. But to design and build an EV from scratch is very expensive, and it's difficult to raise the necessary finances for production.

One more consideration regarding conversions vs. purpose-built is whether you wish to support the big automakers. You can cast an economic vote vote either way by your decision.

In conclusion, the decision to convert or build an EV depends on your situation. For individuals a conversion will possibly result in a lower initial cost than building a car from scratch. This "bottom line" is always important. But such a car will likely use more energy than a purpose-built EV. This means greater grid electricity costs or a larger investment in photovoltaics for solar recharging. For companies planning to produce many EVs for sale, a purpose-built design will undoubtedly be the better choice for the long run. Conversions are a logical, economical step on the way to the better way — designing cars from the beginning to be electric powered.

THE REAL SOLUTION TO POLLUTION, 1992 UPDATE

EDITORIAL SECTION - DON'T READ THIS

Human overpopulation remains the primary threat to the natural environment on which we all depend. As the population increases, it causes more famines, droughts and floods, greater loss of topsoil and fresh-water acquifers, more congested roads with bumper-to-bumper traffic, more garbage and toxic waste, and more plant and animal species lost to extinction.

In their book *The Population Explosion* (New York: Simon & Schuster, 1990), Paul and Anne Erlich often mention the equation I=PAT, where I is negative environmental Impact, P is human Population, A is Affluence (the amount of goods we consume), and T is the technology used to achieve that affluence. (The more technology used, the worse it is for the environment. For example, everyone needs drinking water. Collecting it from rain on the roof is low tech. Driving exhaust-spewing trucks into the semidesert to drill deep wells to drain acquifers, or building a huge system of canals to reroute and dry up the Colorado River is high tech and very destructive.) In this equation, which is an inescapable fact of life on earth, P, A, and T are all multipliers. Increase population or affluence and the environment continues to worsen, in spite of efforts to use more benign technology.

Last year I sent a copy of the ***E.V.D.***, along with letters, to George Bush, Arizona's two senators, and some other politicians. I seem to be an incurable optimist, hoping against reality that such efforts will actually do some good. We need some real leaders, but it's hard to vote "green" when the moneylenders who control politics give us so little to choose from.

I got a letter back from one politician, who wrote that he favors population growth in the U.S. as opposed to growth in "backward countries". (The fallacy there is thinking that the U.S. gets all of its wealth, energy, and materials from within its own borders. The truth is more disturbing, as many U.S. economic policies cause so much misery and poverty for people in other countries.) He also wrote that "human beings can be our greatest asset", and thus population growth should be encouraged. At first it would seem that such a person simply failed third grade math and therefore cannot see that the increasing population thwarts efforts to reduce pollution, and causes other harm. But in reality, it betrays a thought pattern common to many wealthy people. They see humans as commodities; pieces of meat born to serve. Favoring population growth is a way of dehumanizing people. It's concentrating on quantity rather than a real quality of life. ("So what if millions die in poverty and misery, at least there are enough workers left to serve us".) It's as if the "value" of a human is simply to be a living carcass of flesh and blood. That is precisely the demoralizing attitude that fosters heaps of poverty-stricken people huddling around in filth, with no opportunity for a better life.

To the contrary, the important thing is to give each human being the opportunity to reach his or her full potential. This includes proper education, health care, etc. This cannot happen while the population grows faster than facilities can be built, and fresh water acquifers are being depleted *many* times faster than they can be replenished. Rainforests are also being lost because of population pressures so that life-support systems of this finite planet are being thrown out of balance.

To help save the rainforests, we can avoid eating beef, drinking orange juice, and buying tropical hardwoods, as these all contribute to deforestation. The Central American nation of Belize is a beautiful little country, with a relatively good government that is aware of environmental issues and promotes conservation. It's definitely one of the better countries in this regard. But even there the rainforests are being hacked to death to make room for cattle ranching (largely for beef exports) and growing citrus. (Coca Cola, owner of Minute-Maid Orange Juice, has much financial interest in the area.)

But how far do we cut back? Until the earth is simply a giant feedlot for humans who have no more resources to use for their creativity in music, art, or technology? Are we not to enjoy any good-tasting food because it might lead to environmental destruction? Are we all supposed to eat only bread and drink only water so that there's room enough for billions more to have the same kind of existence? Or should we address the human overpopulation problem in a benign way so that each person can have a better and more enjoyable life?

Developing more fuel-efficient cars does no good at all when there will soon be twice as many cars in use, thus multiplying the pollution problem. And, of course, electric cars will do absolutely nothing to alleviate the present gridlock problems on many highways (though at least the air inhaled at those times would be cleaner).

Of course this is not to suggest that merely by achieving and maintaining a reasonable human population that this earth will then be a paradise. It wasn't a paradise 1,000 years ago when the population was much smaller. There is so much injustice and other social issues that must be dealt with. But preoccupation with these must not be allowed to mask the larger threat.

Obviously, reducing birth rates is important. So is reducing our consumption of non-essentials.

Jerry Mander, author of *Four Arguments for the Elimination of Television*, was an advertising executive who realized that his profession led to environmental destruction by creating markets for products where none had existed before. After he left advertising he wrote in his book: "To the capitalist, profit-oriented mind, there is no outrage so great as the existence of some unmediated nook or cranny of creation which has not been converted into a new form which can then be sold for money.... A forest of uncut trees is nonproductive [in the capitalist sense]. A piece of land which has not been built upon is nonproductive. Coal or oil that remains in the ground is nonproductive.... Iron, tungsten, trees, oil, sulfur, jaguars and open space are searched out and transformed because transformation creates economic benefits for the transformers." (New York: William Morrow and Company, Inc., 1978, page 117-118). That's the main reason for the push to "produce", which in reality often means "consume".

I know of one EV salesman who does not own a car. He lives only three miles from work and has no need for such a vehicle. That's a very wholesome approach to environmental problems. If you can get along without a car, so much the better. But if you must drive, it's better to own an EV and recharge it with the sun, if possible. But this does require money, so the transition is necessarily slow.

Long ago big business reversed the axiom "Necessity is the mother of invention", so that invention became the mother of necessity. Now when something is invented, many people feel that they must have it, though they got along fine without it before. For many people the thrill of consumption is not so much having things, as acquiring them. It's a pleasure to get, but the thrill wears off, even when the new item still functions. But instead of falling into the trap set by huge corporations and the big advertising industry that they employ, we can buck the system. Our challenge is to turn the saying around again and find creative ways of doing more with less.

SPECIAL-PURPOSE EVs

SOLAR VEHICLES

At this time solar cars are not practical means of transportation. These vehicles each seat one person in a cramped enclosure. So far, these are each one-of-a-kind prototypes that are built as university or corporate projects. Most are very expensive; some have over $500,000 worth of exotic photovoltaic cells (more efficient than commonly available PVs). The electricity produced by the PVs from sunlight is stored in small batteries on board the vehicle. When the vehicle is at rest in the sunshine, the batteries are constantly being charged. This stored energy allows the car to travel faster than it could if powered directly from the sunlight as it moves.

It's wonderful to think about having a solar powered commuter car that can carry two or four people and have unlimited range provided by free "fuel" during daylight hours. But such a dream is a long way from reality. Though some solar cars are legally roadworthy, remember that they are still expensive research vehicles, not the answer to your present commuting needs. With present technology, a more practical approach to a solar-powered car is to recharge it from a home or business-based solar electricity setup. This allows a much greater array of PV panels to catch the sun's rays. Listed here are just a few of the many solar car projects. Most project organizers are looking for additional funding.

Arizona Horizon Project
Center for Energy Systems Research
Arizona State University
Tempe, Arizona 85287-5806
U.S.A.
PH: 602-965-2896

A.S.U.'s solar-powered vehicle is called the Sun Devil Cruiser. The project cost was estimated at $170,000, including student labor valued at $130,000. This vehicle is powered by a brushless 7.5 kW (10 hp) motor and has lead-acid batteries. It is 6 meters long, 2 meters wide, and weighs 330 kilograms.

Drexel University
College of Engineering
32nd and Chestnut Streets
Philadelphia, Pennsylvania 19104
U.S.A.
PH: 215-895-2210
FAX: 215-895-4929

Drexel University has built two solar powered race vehicles, which they have taken to races and displays. Finley Shapiro and Michel Barsoum are faculty advisers.

New Hampshire Technical Institute
P.O. Box 2039
Institute Drive - Little Hall
Concord, New Hampshire 03302-2039
U.S.A.
PH: 603-225-1885

The New Hampshire Technical Institute has built two prototype electric vehicles. The *SUNTECH* is a solar racing vehicle, while the *SUNGO* is a commuter vehicle based on a conversion. Thomas Hopper and Steve Ryan are faculty advisers, and John Hollins is the technical adviser.

Rose-Hulman Institute of Technology
5500 Wabash Avenue
Terre Haute, Indiana 47803-3999
U.S.A.
PH: 812-877-8495
FAX: 812-877-3198

The Solar Phantom is Rose-Hulman's solar vehicle. This machine has a 3.7 kW (5 hp) motor. The vehicle is 5.6 meters long, and the solar array is 2 meters wide (the body is much narrower). Vehicle empty weight is 148 kilograms. It cost $78,000 to build. Top speed is 42 mph. The Solar Phantom has Silver-Zinc batteries, with a total of 80 cells, manufactured by Eagle Pitcher. It has 722 PV cells manufactured by Arco/Siemens. These produce about 950 watts at 108 volts; maximum voltage is 196.

Stanford Solar Car Project
P.O. Box 8827
Stanford, California 94309-8827
U.S.A.
PH: 415-325-3671
FAX: 415-723-0010

Stanford's newest solar car project is the Sunburner. A unique feature of this design is that it has a concentrator module mounted on top of the driver's compartment. This device uses a parabolic mirror to focus sunlight onto a V-shaped arm mounted above the mirror. This gives a concentration ratio (of sunlight area to PV cell area) of 30:1. This allows a drastic reduction in the cost of the exotic and expensive PV cells. By comparison, GM's Sunraycer had several square meters of gallium-arsenide cells covering its body. This solar array cost over $1,000,000. An equivalent array could be built for about $34,000 on the Sunburner, since only the V-shaped arm on their design would have the solar cells. The mirror and arm unit can be tilted to track the sun. The low-drag body of the Sunburner is constructed of advanced composite FRP materials, having a Nomex honeycomb core sandwiched between layers of carbon fiber.

Sun Luis Project
Department of Mechanical Engineering
California Polytechnic State University
San Luis Obispo, California 93407
U.S.A.
PH: 805-756-1334
FAX: 805-756-6503 (c/o Dr. Moustafa)

Cal Poly's solar race vehicle is the Sun Luis. This vehicle is 1 meter high, 2 meters wide, and 6 meters long. It contains silver-zinc and nickel-cadmium batteries and a flat 8 square meter solar array. Its 15 kW (20 hp) Uniq motor (by Unique Mobility) gives the vehicle a top speed of 62 mph. The empty (curb) weight of the Sun Luis is 213 kilograms. Over the coming year the solar array is to be replaced and the overall vehicle aerodynamics improved.

Cal Poly students are also constructing a second vehicle, the Solstice Solar/Electric Commuter Vehicle (SECV). This is to be a two place safe and practical electric car powered partially by solar energy. It is designed as an urban/suburban commuter vehicle with a range of 80-100 miles per charge. This new design is expected to have an empty weight of 545 kilograms (1,200 lbs), and a cruising speed of 55 mph. The concept is to drive the Solstice to work (30-50 miles), park it in the sun all day, then drive home on the stored solar energy. A full size mock-up has been made and construction of the chassis has begun.

Palmer Industries, Inc.
P.O. Box 707
Endicott, New York 13760
U.S.A.
PH: 800-847-1304
PH: 607-754-1954 (in NY)

Established in 1973, Palmer sells fully assembled electric tricycles as well as kits and electrical components for the customer who wants to convert his own bicycle to electric. Small motors and related equipment is available for those who want an electric assist for the pedal bicycles. One of their fully assembled vehicles is listed below.

PALMER TWOSOME

The Twosome is an electric tricycle with seating for two, side by side. It has forward and reverse, light and horn switch, and other features. The basket behind the seat has a 200 pound capacity. The price is about $3,100.

Seats	2
Length	1.83 m (6 ft 0 in)
Height	0.97 m (3 ft 2 in)
Weight, without batteries	70 kg (155 lbs)
Speed	0 – 23 kph (0 – 14 mph)
Range, with 2 golf cart batteries	80 km (50 miles)

Smiths
658 W. Willow
Enid, Oklahoma 73701
U.S.A.

Merlin Smith offers plans for those who wish to build an electric bicycle. The basic plans cost $12. The bicycle can reach 35 to 40 mph, and has an in-town driving range of about 15 miles, depending on the type of batteries used. The plans include information on parts sources. The motor should cost about $300, and the other items, including various switches, would together cost about another $100. The plans to construct a fiberglass fairing for the body should be available soon. A photo of this bicycle was shown in the Summer 1991 edition of the Directory. Mr. Smith is now also selling plans for a three-wheeled cycle, of which a photo is shown below. The trike has a top speed of 45 - 50 mph. The front end assembly, less wheels, is available for $250 plus shipping and handling.

UFX Enterprises
2900Cedar Grove Road
Conshohocken, Pennsylvania 19428
U.S.A.
PH:h215-828-9830

John Murphy designed the *Sun Cycle* as a personal project. Although no construction plans are currently available for this solar electric moped, Mr. Murphy would be happy to give advice to those who might wish to construct similar vehicles of their own. He can be contacted at the UFX address. The *Sun Cycle* now has four 30-watt solar panels. Two slide out to the rear during recharging, and slide back in for riding. The maximum speed is 34 kph (21 mph) and the range is 40 kilometers (25 miles).

AMERICAS

California Electric Cars, Inc.
1669 Del Monte Boulevard
Seaside, California 93955
U.S.A.
PH: 408-899-2012

The Monterey

California Electric Car's Monterey is a two seat four-wheeled EV. This vehicle has front wheel drive and is available as a complete turn-key car. The battery pack consists of sixteen 6-volt batteries. The pack can be completely recharged in five or six hours from a 220-volt outlet. C.E.C. is offering an introductory price of $19,500 for the Monterey. Options include a hard top, soft top, stereo, and custom wheels. All parts are warranted for one year.

Seats	2
Curb Weight	1,134 kg (2,500 lbs)
Top Speed	113 kph (70 mph)
Range	97 - 176 km (60 - 110 miles)

Dolphin Vehicles
P.O. Box 110215
Campbell, California 95011-0215
U.S.A.
408-734-2052

Vortex

The Vortex is a lightweight three wheeler. Originally powered by an 82 hp Kawasaki engine, the prototype was recently changed to run on electric power. A single drive wheel is located in the rear; the front wheels provide steering. Construction is primarily of wood, foam, and fiberglass, using methods developed for homebuilt aircraft. No kits are available, but the detailed plans list material sources. Many parts and materials may be available locally. The front suspension system, for example, comes from a Triumph Spitfire. Some welding is necessary, primarily for the rear wheel swing arm and the motor mount. Most other parts can be purchased from auto salvage yards or other sources. The prototype has eight 12-volt lead-acid batteries, with a total of 96 volts in the system. A 10 hp Advanced D.C. motor provides traction.

The construction plans for the Vortex are thorough and well illustrated. The set includes thirteen 17" x 22" printed technical drawings and a 64 page construction manual. (The big drawings are helpful.) The price for the plans is $40, which includes shipping and handling in the U.S.A. A poster of the Vortex is available for $12.

Seats	2
Length	3.86 m (12 ft 8 in)
Height	1.04 m (3 ft 5 in)
Wheelbase	2.72 m (8 ft 11 in)
Empty Weight	681 kg (1,500 lbs)
Motor	7.5 kW (10 hp)
Top Speed	97 kph (60 mph)
Range	64 - 97 km (40 - 60 miles)

Doran Motor Company
1728 Bluehaven Drive, Dept. ZEVD
Sparks, Nevada 89431
U.S.A.
702-352-5909

Doran Electric ZEV

The Doran Motor Company sells plans for a three-wheeler that can be built with electric propulsion, which is described here, or powered by an 82 hp Subaru engine. Their electric version uses ten 12.6 volt lead-acid batteries and a 28 hp Advanced DC motor. The ZEV is designed with enough power to make it a truly useful vehicle with decent performance. Range suffers somewhat with that much power and present battery technology. But Doran is confident that better batteries will be available in the not-too-distant future and wants to offer a car that is designed from the beginning to have sufficient performance. This EV has a lightweight foam and fiberglass body over a welded steel frame.

The plans for this attractive vehicle cost $39.95 plus $4.00 postage in the U.S.A. The plans are in the form of a 95-page 8½" x 11" book containing the the working drawings and instructions. A nice color brochure is available for $5.00. A quarterly newsletter is also available; it costs $12.00 per year. Hopefully this vehicle will be put into production, if enough working capital can be raised, with a price tag of about $15,000.

Seats	2
Length	3.66 m (12 ft 0 in)
Height	1.17 m (3 ft 10 in)
Width	1.70 m (5 ft 7 in)
Wheelbase	2.29 m (7 ft 6 in)
Curb Weight	676 kg (1,490 lbs)
Top Speed	129 kph (85 mph)
Acceleration, 0 – 60 mph	10.9 seconds
Range (80% discharge)	61 miles city, 42 freeway

Electric Power Research Institute
3412 Hillview Avenue
P.O. Box 10412
Palo Alto, California 94303
U.S.A.
PH: 415-855-2981

G-Van

The G-Van is an electric van developed by EPRI, Vehma International, Chloride EV Systems, and General Motors Corporation. This vehicle uses much technology from the British GM Griffon, also an electric powered van. The G-Van is expected to have a 30,000 mile battery life. It is estimated that "fuel" costs for the G-Van will be about 4.5 cents per mile, based on .94 kWh/mile and 5 cents/kWh. Many ICE vans have a fuel cost of about 10 cents per mile, based on 10 mpg at $1.00 per gallon. Maintenance costs are also expected to be lower, based on the Griffon track record. Both vehicles use a single speed gear-driven transmission.

Because the G-Van is a conversion of an ICE van, it is quite heavy and not as efficient as a purpose-built electric van could be. Sales so far have been to commercial users only. The production is low, since the vehicles are converted one by one on a small scale. The purchase price is about $50,000.

Seats	7
Length	5.13 m (16 ft 10 in)
Height	2.08 m (6 ft 10 in)
Width	2.01 m (6 ft 7 in)
Overall width with mirrors	2.29 m (7 ft 6 in)
Curb Weight	3,481 kg (7,672 lbs)
Gross Weight	3,901 kg (8,600 lbs)
Wheelbase	3.18 m (10 ft 5 in)
Top Speed	84 kph (52 mph)
Acceleration, 0 – 30 mph	13 seconds
Range, 35 mph constant speed	145 km (90 miles)
Range, simulated city driving	97 km (60 miles)

4E Corporation
4128 Whitsett #104
Studio City, California 91604
U.S.A.
PH: 818-753-8324
FAX: 818-753-2911

EXAR-1

Developed by Edward X. Ramirez, Sr., the EXAR-1 was designed from the beginning to be powered by electricity. Having spent several years developing other EV prototypes, from a two place sports car to an electric minivan (long before the minivan concept was popularized by the Detroit automakers), Ramirez' corporation then set to work on the present vehicle. The body was styled by Pietro Frua, a well-known Italian car designer. Ramirez and his staff had as their goal to design and manufacture a practical electric car that would seat up to five people and have sufficient performance to be a realistic and ecologically better alternative to a petroleum-fueled car. The prototype was completed in 1979, and the plan was to put the vehicle into production in the early 1980s, but sufficient financing was not secured at that time. The prototype was demonstrated to various government and industry organizations in the U.S.A. and Canada.

The EXAR-1 has a steel chassis and two passenger doors. The prototype has a steel body, but production models are to have Kevlar body panels, to reduce weight and corrosion problems, as well as production and repair costs. It is powered by a 19 hp motor. The intended price for each vehicle is $12,000.

Seats	5
Length	5.03 m (16 ft 6 in)
Height	1.26 m (4 ft 1½ in)
Width	1.75 m (5 ft 9 in)
Wheelbase	2.69 m (8 ft 10 in)
Curb Weight	1,361 kg (3,000 lbs)
Gross Weight	1,815 kg (4,000 lbs)
Motor	14 kW (19 hp)
Top Speed	137 kph (85 mph)
Acceleration, 0 – 60 mph	12 seconds
Range @ 55 mph	121 – 161 km (75 –100 miles)

General Motors Corporation
Impact
P.O. Box 302
Bloomfield Hills, Michigan 48303-9923
U.S.A.
PH: 800-253-5328

Impact

The Impact is a relatively new electric car being developed by General Motors. It is not available for purchase at this time. GM began building electric cars in 1916, but of course ICE cars are their primary concern. From the 1960s to the present GM has been building prototype EVs. They never put any into production, though they certainly had the financial resources to do so. Last year they announced their intention to put the Impact, or another EV, into production in the next few years. (Finally!)

With low drag and light weight, the Impact has very impressive performance. It has thirty-two 10-volt Delco-Remy lead-acid batteries connected in series to provide 320 volts. For installation, the batteries slide on a rolling tray down the center of the Impact's chassis. The total battery pack weight is 395 kilograms (870 pounds). Each front wheel is powered by a 57 hp AC induction motor driven through a planetary gear reduction. The two motors develop a total of 114 hp at 6,600 RPM and 94 lb/ft of torque from 0 to 6,000 RPM. The car's projected top speed is over 100 mph, but it is electronically limited to 75 mph. The Impact uses regenerative braking. The drive motors are cooled by a fan forced air system. The cooling-fan speed operates proportionately to the drive motors. Under most driving conditions the fan is turned off, as normal air flow provides adequate ventilation. Heating and air conditioning are provided by a heat pump driven by a 1 horsepower Magnequench motor.

Seats	2
Length	4.14 m (13 ft 7 in)
Height	1.21 m (3 ft 11½ in)
Width	1.73 m (5 ft 8.2 in) Curb
Weight	998 kg (2,200 lbs)
Wheelbase	2.41 m (7 ft 11 in)
Top Speed, electronically limited to	121 kph (75 mph)
Acceleration, 0 – 60 mph	8 seconds
Range @ 89 kph (55 mph)	193 km (120 miles)

Sebring Auto Cycle, Inc.
P.O. Box 1479
Sebring, Florida 33871
U.S.A.
PH: 813-655-2131 FAX: 813-655-0030

Zzipper

The Zzipper is a three-wheeler with two wheels in front and a drive wheel in the rear. It was designed especially for use as a second vehicle, to be towed behind a large recreational vehicle, and using it for errands when the RV is parked. It requires no modifications for towing. It seats two side by side. This vehicle has an aluminum chassis and a lightweight body made of "Royalite 21" plastic. These items are warranted against structural failure for five years. The motor and drive train have a warranty of 12 months or 12,000 miles. Six 12-volt lead-acid batteries provide the energy.

The present owners/management took over the company four years ago. Sebring Vanguard and Commuter Vehicles, two previous company names, operated from the same address and together sold over 4,000 electric cars. The price of the Zzipper is currently about $9,000. Several options are available.

Seats	2
Length	4.11 m (13 ft 6 in)
Height	1.28 m (4 ft 2½ in)
Width	1.32 m (4 ft 4 in)
Wheelbase	2.44 m (8 ft 0 in)
Curb Weight	676 kg (1,490 lbs)
Motor	7.5 kW (10 hp)
Top Speed	over 89 kph (55 mph)
Acceleration, 0 – 50 mph	28 seconds
Range	80 km (50 miles)

Solar Car Corporation
1300 Lake Washington Road
Melbourne, Florida 32935
U.S.A.
PH: 407-254-2997
FAX: 407-254-4773

Festiva

The Solar Car Corporation offers a Ford Festiva conversion that is available in two configurations - electric and solar electric. Each retrofit vehicle has regenerative braking, solar-assisted charge modes, and a built-in battery charger. They also feature modular construction to facilitate maintenance and repair. The solar option can extend the driving range for about 10 miles on a sunny day. An additional advantage of this system is to extend the life of the batteries by having them constantly trickle-charged during sunny conditions. The battery box is cut into the floor and the frame is reinforced. This gives the vehicle a low center of gravity for better handling. The Festiva has ten 12-volt lead-acid batteries, though other battery types are available as an option. The pure electric model sells for $17,500, while the solar electric vehicle costs $22,500. The price of either model is reduced by $2,000 for those who bring in their own used Festiva.

Seats	2
Wheelbase	2.29 m (7 ft 6 in)
Ground Clearance	15 cm (6 in)
Curb Weight	998 - 1,043 kg (2,200 - 2,300 lbs)
Gross Weight	1,361 kg (3,000 lbs)
Battery Weight	318 kg (700 lbs)
Motor	12 kW (16 hp, 120 VDC)
Top Speed	105 kph (65 mph)
Range	40 - 97 km (25 - 60 miles)

Chevrolet/GMC S-10/S-15

Solar Car Corporation's latest entry in the field of electric vehicles is a multi-purpose pick-up truck. This vehicle also features modular construction for easy serviceability. A manual transmission is available as standard equipment, though an automatic transmission is available as an option. (This will reduce mileage by 10 to 20 percent.) The standard clutch assembly is retained to keep the driving smooth. This pick-up uses twenty 6-volt batteries, providing a total system voltage of 120 volts. Solar Car Corp. says that this would make an excellent fleet vehicle with low maintenance. Several custom body options are available, including a camper-top with a solar array. The price of the basic vehicle, without the solar assist option, is $19,500. This price is reduced by $2,000 for those who bring in their own used pick-up.

Seats	2, plus cargo area
Wheelbase	2.74 m (9 ft 0 in)
Gross Weight	1,588 kg (3,500 lbs)
Motor	21 kW (28 hp)
Top Speed	113 kph (70 mph)
Range	64 - 113 km (40 - 70 miles)

Solar Electric Engineering, Inc.
116 Fourth Street
Santa Rosa, California 95401-6212
U.S.A.
PH: 707-542-1990
FAX: 707-542-4358

Solar Electric has sold many electric cars in the past few years. They carry some used EVs in stock and also convert three ICE car models to EVs. These are the Ford Escort and Tempo, and the Pontiac Fiero. These vehicles can be purchased already converted, or a customer can bring in his own car for conversion. Solar Electric also builds its own EV based on the Fiero chassis. They also offer kits and components for those who wish to do their own conversions.

Escort

Solar Electric's electric conversion of the Escort costs $15,700. This car can reach up to about 65 mph. At slower speeds, driving range is about 60 miles. A solar-assist package option is available on this and all other cars offered by Solar Electric. With this option, flexible PV panels with a total power output of 200 watts are installed on the roof and hood of the vehicle. This extends the range slightly and increases battery life. When the car is parked in the sun, the batteries receive a constant charge from the solar cells.

Electron-One

Called, the Electron-One, Solar Electric's Ford Tempo conversion also costs $15,700. This car has a manual transmission and solid-state controller. The lead-acid battery pack can have a system voltage of 96 to 108 volts.

Seats	5
Speed	89 – 97 kph (50 – 60 miles)
Range	56 – 80 km (35 – 50 miles)

Electron-Two

The Electron-Two is a Fiero conversion, also with a manual transmission and solid state controller. The base price is $16,200.

Seats	2
Speed	89 – 105 kph (55 – 65 mph)
Range	56 – 89 km (35 – 55 miles)

Electron-Three

The Electron-Three is an electric van. With the solar option, this vehicle sells for $29,700.

Destiny *2000*

The Destiny is a two seat custom sports car based on the Fiero chassis. It has a lightweight fiberglass body and comes standard with a solar-assist package. This car made a brief appearance in the movie *Naked Gun 2½* (by Paramount Pictures). The current price of the Destiny is $28,500. Several have already been sold.

Seats	2
Speed	97 - 113 kph (60 - 70 mph)
Range	64 -97 km (40 - 60 miles)

Solectria
27 Jason Street
Arlington, Massachusetts 02174
U.S.A.
PH: 617-894-6670
FAX: 617-894-9522

Force

Solectria's Force is a new four place EV conversion based on the Suzuki Swift (or Chevrolet Geo). A two place version of the same basic car is also available, offering slightly higher performance and more range. The specifications shown below are for the four place vehicle. Standard equipment on this car include an on-board 110-volt AC battery charger, and an electric heater. The Force has a single speed automatic transmission. Options include air conditioning, cruise control, and a roof-mounted solar panel system (150 watts) to assist in battery charging. The Force should be available by this time. The price, new, is expected to be about $25,000.

Seats	4
Length	3.71 m (12 ft 2 in)
Height	1.33 m (4 ft 4½ in)
Width	1.57 m (5 ft 2 in)
Wheelbase	2.27 m (7 ft 4½ in)
Curb Weight	972 kg (2,142 lbs)
Top Speed	97 kph (60 mph)
Acceleration, 0 – 30 mph	8 seconds
Acceleration, 0 – 60 mph	21 seconds
Range	97 km (60 miles)

Specialty Vehicle Manufacturing Corporation
12222 Woodruff Avenue
Downey, California 90241
U.S.A.
PH: 213-803-5589
FAX: 213-803-4044
President - Don Duffy
General Manager - Rich Krantz

Trolley Series 3000

The Series 3000 trolley is a battery-powered vehicle with the classic appearance of the people-movers of nearly a century ago. This vehicle has a stainless steel structure with a fiberglass skin and features tinted drop sash windows. For handicapped riders there is a wheel chair position with a flip down seat. A 32 hp brushless permanent magnet motor is used with the 144 volt battery system. The trolley has power steering and power brakes. A significant characteristic of this design is that many people will gladly ride a trolley with classic looks, though they might have no interest in boarding a transit bus. The trolley is, of course, intended for sale to commercial operators.

Passenger Capacity	21 passengers seated
Length	6.65 m (21 ft 10 in)
Height	2.79 m (9 ft 2 in)
Width	2.06 m (6 ft 9 in)
Wheelbase	2.92 m (9 ft 7 in)
Gross Weight	5,898 kg (13,000 lbs)
Motor	24 kW (32 hp)
Top Speed	56 kph (35 mph)
Range	80 - 145 km (50 - 90 miles)

Unique Mobility, Inc.
3700 South Jason Street
Englewood, Colorado 80110
U.S.A.
PH: 303-761-2137

M-91

Unique Mobility is an engineering company that began its electric vehicle development program in 1973. By 1982 they had built fifty fiberglass electric passenger cars. The Electrek Uncar had a 24 kW (32 hp) motor and a top speed of 75 mph. Unfortunately, this vehicle is no longer available.

In 1988 Unique and Alcan Aluminum Ltd. began a joint program to develop an advanced electric powertrain system. Recently they introduced a lead-acid battery EV based on a Chrysler minivan. This vehicle, now designated the M-91, uses a 12 hp engine to drive a 5 kW generator to extend the vehicle's range to 100 miles. Using natural gas, liquid propane, or methanol, the engine-generator produces very little pollution. The M-92 has eighteen 12-volt batteries, and the electrical system uses 108 volts. An on-board charger plugs into a 240-volt AC power outlet for overnight charging. Recharging takes six hours.

We have received no recent news of this vehicle, and the status of this project is uncertain.

Seats	7
Motor	60 kW (80 hp)
Top Speed	113 kph (70 mph)
Acceleration, 0 – 30 mph	8.5 seconds

ASSOCIATIONS, NEWSLETTERS

American Hydrogen Association
219 S. Siesta Lane, Suite 101
Tempe, Arizona 85281
U.S.A.
PH: 602-921-0433
FAX: 602-967-6601
President - Roy McAlister
V.P. of Engineering - Herb Hayden
Dir. of Racing - Demetri Wagner
Ass'n. to promote education and use of hydrogen. $15/yr. regular membership, incl. bimonthly newsletter. Also publishes quarterly journal. Demonstrations of hydrogen conversions on many engine types. Sells books on hydrogen use.

Arizona Solar Energy Association
P.O. Box 26
Scottsdale, Arizona 85252
U.S.A.
PH: 602-965-7608
State Chairman - Mike Walters
Ass'n. to promote use of solar energy. $6/yr. for bimonthly newsletter, *Under the Sun.*

Battery Council International
401 N. Michigan Avenue
Chicago, Illinois 60611
U.S.A.
PH: 312-644-6610
FAX: 312-321-6869
Trade ass'n. for mfrs. of lead-acid batteries and related products. Sells Several publications incl. a Battery *Service Manual; Technical Manual;* & *Battery Replacement Data Book.*

Clean Air Revival
55 New Montgomery, Suite 424
San Francisco, California 94105
U.S.A.
PH: 415-495-0495
FAX: Same as above
C.A.R. is a not-for-profit educational corp. dedicated to providing hands on experience with EVs and R.E. technology, encourages public participation. Organizes solar expo, EV races, and other events.

Denver Electric Vehicle Council
2940 13th Street
Boulder, Colorado 80304
U.S.A.
PH: 303-442-6566
DEVC is a not-for-profit educational organization for the promotion of EVs. Only $10/yr. regular membership, incl. monthly newsletter. Approx. 200 members.

Doran Motor Company
1728 Bluehaven Drive, Dept. ZEVD
Sparks, Nevada 89431
U.S.A.
PH: 702-352-5909
Quarterly newsletter for $12/yr. Covers primarily Doran's own EV design with helpful hints to ease construction. Also contains info. on other EVs.

Earthmind
P.O. Box 743
Mariposa, California 95338
U.S.A.
PH: 213-396-1527
Publisher - Michael Hackleman
Bimonthly magazine *Alternative Transportation News*. The biggest periodical dealing with EVs and other benign transportation. Six issues/yr. for $20. Add $6 in Canada; inquire about rates elsewhere.

Eastern Electric Vehicle Club
P.O. Box 717
Valley Forge, Pennsylvania 19482
U.S.A.
Dues are $12/yr. as they have been for 11 years; includes monthly newsletter.

Electric Auto Association
1249 Lane Street
Belmont, California 94002
U.S.A.
PH: 415-591-6698
The original EV ass'n., with 6 chapters in California, and one each in Arizona, Massachusetts, Nevada, New Jersey, Texas, and Washington. Membership: $25/yr. incl. big monthly newsletter.

Electric Grand Prix Corporation
6 Gateway Circle
Rochester, New York 14624-4415
U.S.A.
PH: 716-889-1229
President - Paul Heaney
Test EV related equipment and publish results. Write critical analysis of articles and publications related to EV development. Publish *Electric Grand Prix* quarterly. No charge, donations welcome.

Electric Vehicle Association of Canada
395 Matheson Boulevard East
Mississauga, Ontario N4Z 2H2
CANADA
PH: 416-890-1846
FAX: 416-890-5769
President - J.W. Kerr
Membership dues include high-quality quarterly publication, *Electric Propulsion*. $50 in Canada, $60 U.S.A., $70 elsewhere.

Electric Vehicle Association of Greater Washington (EVA/DC)
9140 Centerway Road
Gaithersburg, Maryland 20879
U.S.A.
PH: 301-231-3990 (voice mail)
President - David E. Goldstein
V.P. - David Peaslee
Formed in 1980 as an Electric Auto Ass'n. chapter for Washington, D.C. area, now reforming with new membership drive. Please leave message on "voice mail".

Electric Vehicle Association of San Diego (EVAOSD)
9011 Los Coches Road
Lakeside, California 92040
U.S.A.
PH: 619-443-3017
President - Ron Larrea
V.P. - Gary Jackson
Sec./Treasurer - Ken McDonald
Editor - Tom Steinke
Librarian - Bob Paget
Meets monthly, 20-30 people attend each meeting. Dues: $25/yr. includes Elec. Auto Ass'n. national newsletter and EVAOSD local newsletter.

Electric Vehicle Association of Southern California (EVAOSC)
P.O. Box 16
Ontario Downtown
Ontario, California 91762-9998
U.S.A.
PH: 714-624-3068
Ass'n that promotes the use of EVs and aids individuals in the purchase or construction of their own. Encourages gov't. legislation in favor of EVs. Membership: $15/yr., incl. monthly newsletter.

Electric Vehicle Council of Ottawa (EVCO)
Box 4044 Station "E"
Ottawa, Ontario K1S 5B1
CANADA
PH: 613-722-9939 (Rick Lane)
President - Dick Bonnycastle
Secretary - Richard Lane
Treasurer - Allan Grander
Membership: $20/yr. incl. newsletter, *EV Circuit*. Also offers consultation services.

Electric Vehicle Development Corporation
20823 Stevens Creek Boulevard, #440
Cupertino, California 95014
U.S.A.
PH: 408 253-5262
FAX: 408-253-9704
Trade ass'n. of electric utilities, mfg. companies, and gov't. agencies. Publishes monthly newsletter.

Electric Vehicle News
1911 N. Fort Meyer Drive
Suite 703
Arlington, Virginia 22209
U.S.A.
PH: 703-276-9093
FAX: 703-524-4093
Monthly EV newsletter, $30/yr.

Electric Vehicle Progress
215 Park Avenue South, Suite 1301
New York, New York 10003-1603
U.S.A.
PH: 212-228-0246
FAX: 212-228-0376
Publishes *Electric Vehicle Progress*. 24 issues/yr. for $327/yr.

Electronic Transportation Design
P.O. Box 111
Yachats, Oregon 97498
U.S.A.
PH: 503-547-3506
FAX: 503-547-3539
Design Engineer - Clarence W. Ellers
Publisher of *World Electric Transportation.* $33 for 12 issues.

EV Consultants
327 Central Park West
New York, New York 10025
U.S.A.
PH: 212-222-0160
Publisher - Edward A. Campbell
Publishes monthly *Alternate Energy Transportation Newsletter.* $200/yr.

Northeast Sustainable Energy Association
23 Ames Street
Greenfield, Massachusetts 01301
U.S.A.
PH: 413-774-6051
FAX: 413-774-6053
Not-for-profit educational sustainable energy ass'n. Organizes annual May Tour de Sol to promote solar & elec. vehicle development and use. Holds annual Solar & EV Symposium. Publishes *Northeast Sun* quarterly. Membership: $35/yr.

Northern California Solar Energy Ass'n.
P.O. Box 3008
Berkeley, California 94703
U.S.A.
PH: 408-277-5533
FAX: 408-277-3606
President - Mary Tucker
Secretary/Pres. - Robin Mitchell
Individual membership: $20/yr. incl. quarterly newsletter, *Northern California Sun.*

Oregon Electric Vehicle Association
P.O. Box 347
Amity, Oregon 97101
U.S.A.
PH: 503-835-1212
FAX: 503-835-8901
New EV ass'n.

SAE International
400 Commonwealth Drive
Warrendale, Pennsylvania 15096-0001
U.S.A.
PH: 412-772-7129
FAX: 412-776-2103
Society of Automotive Engineers "For Advancing Mobility Land, Sea, Air and Space".

Solar and Electric Racing Association
11811 North Tatum Boulevard
Suite 3031
Phoenix, Arizona 85028-1621
U.S.A.
PH: 602-953-6672
FAX: 602-953-7733
Organizes SERA 500 annual racing event for EVs and solar cars, to promote knowledge and awareness of EVs, and to do for EVs what Indy 500 has done for ICE cars.

Solar Energy Collection
Daniel E. Noble Science and Engineering Library
Arizona State University
Tempe, Arizona 85287-1506
U.S.A.
PH: 602-965-7608
FAX: 602-965-0883
Library special collection on solar and other renewable energy, EVs.

Solar Energy Expo & Rally
733 South Main Street
Suite 234
Willits, California 95490
U.S.A.
PH: 707-459-1256
Annual event for the promotion of R.E. and conservation. Solar /Electric vehicle races.

Solar Mind
759 South State, #81
Ukiah, California 95482
U.S.A.
PH: 707-468-0878
Publisher - Joe Stevenson
Bimonthly newsletter/magazine on R.E. and EVs. $25/yr. for six issues.

South Central Electric Vehicle Consortium
238 Wisenbaker Building
Texas A & M University
College Station, Texas 77843
U.S.A.
PH: 409-845-8281
FAX: 409-845-9287
Manager - William Craven
Exec. Director - David Swan
Ass'n., research & consultation on EVs.

U.S. Department of Energy
National Appropriate Technology
Assistance Service (NATAS)
P.O. Box 2525
Butte, Montana 59702-2525
U.S.A.
PH: 800-428-2525
The U.S. D.O.E. has many offices. The two listed here may be able to provide some additional information on EVs.

U.S. Department of Energy
Electric and Hybrid Propulsion Division,
Transportation Systems
1000 Independence Avenue, SW
Washington, DC 20585
U.S.A.
PH: 202-586-2198
FAX: 202-586-8134

The Honda CRX is an excellent candidate for conversion to electric power, and several are now operating by that means. Aeronautical engineer Molt Taylor has another idea. With much experience as a designer, builder, and pilot of flying cars, he decided a few years ago that the CRX would be ideal for that purpose. Here's a photo of a model of his proposed design. It's not electric, but maybe it could use hydrogen.

BATTERIES

Concorde Battery Corporation
2009 W. San Bernardino Road
West Covina, California 91760
U.S.A.
PH: 818-962-4006
Mfr. of lead-acid batteries primarily for aircraft use.

Electrochimica Corporation
20 Kelly Court
Menlo Park, California 94025
U.S.A.
PH: 415-327-8600
Mfr. of Nickel-Zinc batteries for EVs. Custom design and fabrication work only.

Trojan

THE DEEP CYCLE CHAMPS

For All Your Battery Needs

ON HIGHWAY ELECTRIC VEHICLES

** Standard EV * Hybrid EV/RV * Solar EV*

OFF-ROAD ELECTRIC VEHICLES

** Golf Cars * Lifts * Hoists*
** Floor Machines*

Trojan is a full-line manufacturer of Automotive, Marine, Commercial, Farm, Garden Tractor and Industrial batteries.

Trojan
The Better Battery

TROJAN BATTERY COMPANY
12380 Clark Street • Santa Fe Springs, CA 90670 • (213) 946-8381
5194 Minola Drive • Lithonia, GA 30038 • (404) 981-8674
Outside California (800) 423-6569

Exide Corporation
645 Penn Street
P.O. Box 14205
Reading, Pennsylvania 19612-4205
U.S.A.
PH: 215-378-0600
FAX: 215-378-0616
Mfr. of lead-acid batteries suitable for EVs.

Pacific West Supply
P.O. Box 347
Amity, Oregon 97101
U.S.A.
PH: 503-835-1212
FAX: 503-835-8901
Gen. Mgr. - Lon Gillas
Battery retailer, and mfr. of reconditioned Ni-Cad batteries.

Rolls Battery Engineering
8 Proctor Street
P.O. Box 671
Salem, Massachusetts 01970
U.S.A.
PH: 508-745-3333
FAX: 508-748-8956
Consultant - John J. Surratte
Mfr. of deep cycle lead-acid EV batteries with heavy plate construction. Also mfrs. autom. voltage regulated battery chargers.

Saft Nife Inc.
251 Industrial Boulevard
P.O. Box 7366
Greenville, North Carolina 27835-7366
U.S.A.
PH: 919-830-1600
FAX: 919-752-0057
Executive V.P. - Arne O. Nilsson
Nat. Sales Mgr EV & AGV - Michael Dodge
Mfr. of Nickel-Iron and Nickel-Cadmium batteries for EV propulsion.

Skyline Engineering
P.O. Box 134
Temple, New Hampshire 03084
U.S.A.
PH: 603-878-1600
FAX: 603-878-4643
President - Dr. Robert Wills
Distributor of Fiber Nickel-Cadmium batteries for EV propulsion.

Tauber Electronics, Inc.
4901 Morena Boulevard
Suite 314
San Diego, California 92117
U.S.A.
PH: 619-274-7242
FAX: 619-274-2220
Owner - Bob Tauber
Sales Manager - Ed Hoscoe
Sales Engineer - Ron Santos
Distributor of batteries; many brand names, types, and sizes. In business 20 years, employ 36 people.

Teledyne Battery Products
840 West Brockton Avenue
P.O. Box 7950
Redlands, California 92375
U.S.A.
PH: 714-793-3131
800-456-0070
FAX: 714-793-5818
Mfr. of Gill batteries. Also researching possibilities for mfg. EV batteries.

Trojan Battery Company
12380 Clark Street
Santa Fe Springs, California 90670
U.S.A.
PH: 213-946-8381
213-521-8215
800-423-6569
FAX: 213-941-6038
Large mfr. of lead-acid batteries for EVs, golf carts, etc. Does *not* sell retail. Trojan batteries are available at many automotive parts stores. *See ad on previous page.*

U.S. Battery Manufacturing Company
1675 Sampson Avenue
Corona, California 91719
U.S.A.
PH: 714-371-8090
800-695-0945
FAX: 714-371-4158
Mfr. of lead-acid batteries suitable for EV propulsion. See additional company listing on next page.

U.S. Battery Manufacturing Company
653 Industrial Park Drive
P.O. Box 649
Evans, Georgia 30809
U.S.A.
PH: 404-868-0532
800-522-0945
FAX: 404-860-9342
President & CEO - John Anderson
Mfr. of lead-acid batteries suitable for EV propulsion.

Voltmaster Company, Inc.
Box 288
Corydon, Iowa 50060
U.S.A.
PH: 515-872-2044
FAX: 515-872-2664
Mfr. of lead-acid batteries, SLI and deep cycle types, suitable for EVs.

Yuasa-Exide, Inc.
9728 Alburtis Avenue
P.O. Box 3748
Santa Fe Springs, California 90670
U.S.A.
PH: 213-949-4266
800-423-4667
FAX: 213-949-5527
President - P. Michael Ehlerman
V.P. Sales & Mktg. - Les Biggins
Mktg. Analyst - Andrew L. Foss
Mfr. of lead-acid batteries for EVs.

The electric vehicle rally starts tomorrow and we have to show the polluters what we can do. Let's "re-volt!"

BOOKS

The following companies and organizations publish books pertaining to EVs. In this edition of the Directory we are no longer listing those who are retailers only (with one exception), because they are too numerous. With most, if not all, of these titles you can order directly from the publisher. Many of the retailers listed in the **Renewable Energy Products** section also carry a good selection of books on EVs, including those titles listed here. Another good idea is to go to your local and/or chain bookstores and ask for some of these titles by name. If they don't stock such titles, ask them why and give them the names and addresses of the publishers listed here. They can help the environment, themselves, and the publishers of these useful books by stocking them in their inventory. There are two more rather new general titles on EVs of which I'm aware. My attempts to contact the authors regarding the latest prices brought no response, so I don't know about the availability of those books.

Battery Council International
401 North Michigan Avenue
Chicago, Illinois 60611
U.S.A.
PH: 312-644-6610
FAX: 312-321-6869
Publishes *Battery Replacement Data Book; Battery Service Manual,* and other various articles.

Electro Automotive
P.O. Box 1113-S
Felton, California 95018-1113
U.S.A.
PH: 408-429-1989
Publisher and retailer of *Convert It* by Michael P. Brown with Shari Prange. This is a step by step guide to converting an ICE car into an EV. $35 plus postage.

Electronic Transportation Design
P.O. Box 111
Yachats, Oregon 97498
U.S.A.
PH: 503-547-3506
FAX: 503-547-3539
Design Engineer - Clarence W. Ellers
Publishes *Electric Vehicle Conversion Manual.* 1991 Edition: $33.

KTA Services
12531 Breezy Way
Orange, California 92669
U.S.A.
PH: 714-639-9799
Electrical Engr. - Ken Koch
Publisher of EV articles, EV book retailer.

Real Goods Trading Corporation
966 Mazzoni Street
Ukiah, California 95482
U.S.A.
PH: 707-468-9214
800-762-7325 (orders only)
FAX: 707-468-0301
Retailer of books on renewable energy and EVs. Publishes annual *Alternative Energy Sourcebook*, primarily a catalog of supplies they offer, has 16 page chapter on EVs.

John Roby
3703 Nassau Drive
San Diego, California 92115
U.S.A.
PH: 619-583-4264
FAX: 619-460-4190
Retailer of large selection of books and articles. Most titles drop-shipped. List #26 has about 300 titles on R.E. and EVs; List #206 has 800 titles on structural materials, incl. FRP composites. Each list costs $2.

SAE International
400 Commonwealth Drive
Warrendale, Pennsylvania 15096-0001
U.S.A.
PH: 412-776-4970
FAX: 412-776-0790
Publishes *Electric Vehicle Technology* ($47 postpaid) and other books and articles on EVs and alternative fuels. Primarily for engineers.

Spirit Publications
Box 23417
Tucson, Arizona 85734
U.S.A.
PH: 602-822-2030
Publisher of *Electric Vehicle Directory.* Wholesale and retail sales.

3E Vehicles
P.O. Box 19409
San Diego, California 92119
U.S.A.
President – Paul R. Schipps
Publisher of EV conversion books.

Bill Williams
P.O. Box 1548
Cupertino, California 95015
U.S.A.
Author and publisher of *Guide to Electric Auto Conversion,* Now in its fourth edition ($19.95 postpaid in U.S.A.), and *EV Battery Evaluation Report* ($7.00 ppd. in U.S.A.)

KTA SERVICES

12531 BREEZY WAY ORANGE, CA 92669
714/639-9799 or 714/821-2000 X5396

Established in 1984, KTA SERVICES caters to electric vehicle hobbyists and manufacturers by supplying EV components, publications, and design/consulting services. We are, at last, a complete supplier of EV components....everything you need except for the batteries. All components we recommend and sell have been selected with safety and reliability foremost in mind. All components have been proof-tested in electric vehicles. All components are new, competitively-priced, and come with full manufacturer's warrantees. We proudly stock the following:

*CURTIS-PMC Motor Controllers
*ADVANCED DC Series-Wound Motors
*ALBRIGHT ENGINEERING Contactors
*GENERAL ELECTRIC Circuit Breakers
*BUSSMAN & RELIANCE Safety Fuses
*SEVCON DC-DC Converters
*K & W ENGINEERING Onboard Chargers
*An ever-growing lineup of EV Publications
*CURTIS-PMC Throttle Pots
*CURTIS INSTRUMENTS Battery 'Fuel' Gauges
*KTA SERVICES' Expanded-Scale Meters
*DELTEC Meter Shunts
*EVCC Adapter Plates & Hubs
*CAROL Ultra-flexible Welding Cable
*THOMAS & BETTS Welding Cable Lugs
*Battery Cables custom-made to spec.

You can purchase your components from us with the confidence of knowing that we specialize in user-friendly customer service. With 10 years of EV experience and engineering expertise, we can answer just about any EV question you can come up with. Additionally, we offer engineering services:

*Complete System Quotations (free)
*Project Overview with Schematic & Recommendations
*Project Consulting/Engineering Design
*Computer-based EV Performance Predictions

Call or write us for your EV needs. For a COMPONENTS & PUBLICATIONS CATALOG, send $5.00 (refundable).

COMPOSITE FRP STRUCTURAL MATERIALS

For homebuilt and custom built electric cars, composite fiber–reinforced plastic structural materials developed for homebuilt aircraft offer great advantages. Among the benefits are corrosion resistance, ease of constructing compound curves and aerodynamic shapes, smooth surfaces, ease of repairs, etc. Using exotic and expensive materials such as Nomex honeycomb, and Kevlar and Graphite fabrics, can also allow lighter structures than are possible with steel or aluminum. Such a weight saving advantage can increase vehicle performance, carrying capacity, range, or a combination of all three. An additional advantage is the capability to construct energy–absorbing cells that deform on impact in the event of a collision.

Most composite FRP structures consist of a core material, such as a plastic foam (Styrofoam, Urethane, etc.) or plywood. This core is then coated with a fabric (fiberglass, Kevlar, graphite, or other material) and an epoxy or polyester matrix system. There are environmental concerns with many of these materials. Most are derived from petrochemicals, and the manufacturing processes are toxic to varying degrees. Hopefully the larger corporations with adequate financing will be encouraged by market pressures to develop more environmentally benign materials and processes.

Remember that there are tradeoffs. Metal, as used in conventional cars, is at least recyclable, though not renewable. This is a great advantage. But in cold climates the steel in many vehicles rusts quickly because of salt poured on the roads in winter. This results in the vehicle being removed from service sooner than it might otherwise need, and it's replaced with a new car. Affluent and consumption–oriented lifestyles are very destructive to the environment. So, keeping an older car in service longer is a desirable alternative. Composite structures can help accomplish this, and in regard to this point they are better for the environment. Then again, the lighter empty weight of a car built with composite materials allows the vehicle to travel more miles for a given amount of energy, which is obviously desirable as well.

Aluminum, though, also deserves careful consideration. For many decades most aircraft, from two place sport planes thru commercial airliners have been built primarily of aluminum. Though composites are now the favored choice for high performance (250 to 300 mph cruise speed) homebuilt aircraft, several fast designs are built of aluminum, to challenge the idea that composites are the only way to go. The fact that aluminum is so easily recyclable (and decent prices are paid for scrap aluminum) make this an attractive structural material as well. When an aluminum vehicle is smashed, the base material can be reused to make another car. Reclaiming fiber–reinforced plastics is much more difficult.

It would be good to see some life cycle analyses made of these different materials to get a better picture of the overall environmental impacts they make. Meanwhile, here is a listing of some companies that offer fiber–reinforced plastic materials.

Aerospace Composite Products
P.O. Box 16621
Irvine, California 92714
U.S.A.
PH: 714–250–1107
FAX: 714–250–0307
Mfr. and retailer of graphite plates and rods, composite panels, and custom work. Primarily for radio–controlled aircraft and cars, though some products may be suitable for larger projects.

Aircraft Plywood Manufacturing, Inc.
620 Thirteenth Street
P.O. Box 133
Highland, Illinois 62249
U.S.A.
PH: 618–654–4323
Mfr. of high quality plywood suitable for aircraft and vehicle structures.

Alexander Aeroplane Company
900 S. Pine Hill Road
Griffin, Georgia 30223
U.S.A.
PH: 404-228-3815
FAX: 404-228-2329
Large supplier of composite materials, tools, and homebuilt aircraft supplies. 80 page catalog: $3.

Chem-Tech, Inc.
4669 Lander Road
Chagrin Falls, Ohio 44022
U.S.A.
PH: 216-248-0770
Mfr. and retailer of epoxies and structural adhesives.

Clark Foam Products
25887 Crown Valley Parkway
South Laguna, California 92677
U.S.A.
PH: 714-582-1431
FAX: 714-582-5085
Mfr. of rigid polyurethane foam. Uses CO_2, rather than CFCs, as a blowing agent.

Clark-Schwebel Fiber Glass Corporation
5 Corporate Park Drive
Box 851 C
White Plains, New York 10603
U.S.A.
PH: 914-694-9090
FAX: 914-694-9096
World's largest mfr. of industrial fiberglass. Also mfrs. Kevlar, Spectra, and Quartz fabrics. Also has plants in Belgium and Japan.

Hexcel Corporation
Administrative Office
11555 Dublin Boulevard
Dublin, California 94568
U.S.A.
PH: 415-828-4200
415-828-4256
FAX: 415-828-7101
Mgr. Honeycomb Mktg. - John Porter
Mgr. Adv. Compsts Mktg. - Jim Bumgarner
Mfr. of Safe-T-Poxy resin systems and honeycomb cores made from aluminum, steel, fiberglass, graphite, and aramid fibers. Also mfrs. other FRP materials.

Textile Products, Inc.
2512 W. Woodland Drive
Anaheim, California 92801
U.S.A.
PH: 714-761-0401
FAX: 714-761-2928
Mfr. of graphite fabrics.

Wicks Aircraft Supply
410 Pine Street
Highland, Illinois 62249
U.S.A.
PH: 618-654-7447
FAX: 618-654-6253
Large retailer of composite materials, plywood, spruce, and tools. 410 page catalog: $6.00

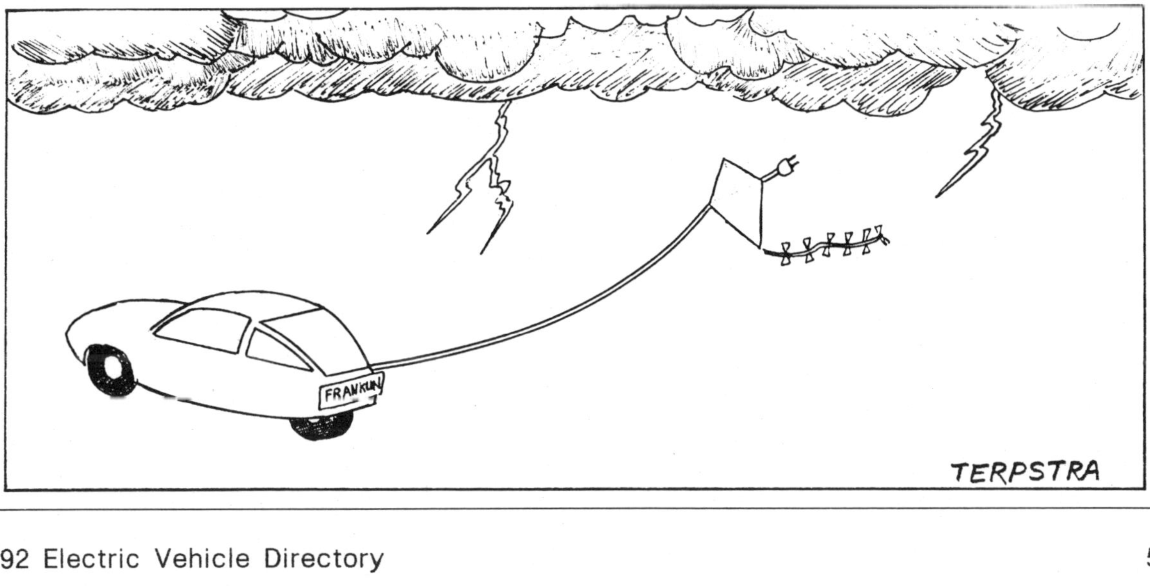

CONSULTANTS

The following companies and organizations offer consultation services with regard to EVs. Such services may include advice regarding a specific proposal for an EV project, performance predictions, information of various kinds, and other help.

Amerigon Incorporated
425 E. Huntington Drive
Monrovia, California 91016
U.S.A.
PH: 818-305-1100
FAX: 818-305-1106
President – Lon Bell
V.P. Mktg. & Planning – Fredrick J. Clarey
Research and development of commercial EVs.

Electric Motor Cars
4301 Kingfisher
Houston, Texas 77035
U.S.A.
PH: (713) 729-8668
Consultation, conversion, repair.

Electric Vehicles, Inc.
2736 Winfield Drive
Mountain View, California 94040
U.S.A.
PH: 415-964-3974
EV consultation and R & D.

Electric Vehicles of America, Inc.
P.O. Box 59
Maynard, Massachusetts 01754
U.S.A.
PH: 508-897-9393
FAX: 508-897-1731
EV consulting, strategic planning for EV use by utilities, associations and businesses.

Electro Automotive
P.O. Box 1113-S
Felton, California 95018-1113
U.S.A.
PH: 408-429-1989
Consultation on EV projects, also has large stock of EV components.

Electronic Transportation Design (ETD)
P.O. Box 111
Yachats, Oregon 97498
U.S.A.
PH: 503-547-3506
FAX: 503-547-3539
Design and prototyping. Hybrid-electric patent license for sale.

Electrotek Concepts, Inc.
P.O. Box 16548
Chattanooga, Tennessee 37416
U.S.A.
PH: 615-622-EVTF
FAX: 615-629-4097
Independent agency providing testing and evaluation of EVs & components, measuring drivetrain efficiency, etc. Publishes reports with data.

Interesting Transportation, Inc.
2362 Southridge Drive
Palm Springs, California 92264
U.S.A.
PH: 619-327-2864
President – Frank A. Kelly
EV consultation and R & D.

KTA Services
12531 Breezy Way
Orange, California 92669
U.S.A.
PH: 714-639-9799
Proprietor, Engineer – Ken Koch
Proprietor – Judy Koch
Conversions, consultation, EV maintenance and repair, EV performance predictions, analysis, electrical design.

Program Development Associates (of MD)
9140 Centerway Road
Gaithersburg, Maryland 20879
U.S.A.
PH: 301-869-4954
President – David Goldstein
Repair and maintenance of EVs, consulting services for fleets, utilities, and local governments.

U.F.X. Enterprises
290 Cedar Grove Road
Conshohocken, Pennsylvania 19428
U.S.A.
PH: 215-828-9830
Professional engineering and fabrication services relating to EVs and prototypes.

It looks like the ICE Age is almost over.

CONVERSION SERVICES/EV REPAIR

E–Motion
515 West 15th Street
McMinnville, Oregon 97128
U.S.A.
PH: 503–434–4332
Converts lightweight sports cars to electric power.

Electric Auto Crafters
2S 643 Nelson Lake Road
Batavia, Illinois 60510
U.S.A.
PH: 708–879–0207 (residence)
Owner – John Stockberger
Conversions, EV parts.

Electric Motor Cars
4301 Kingfisher
Houston, Texas 77035
U.S.A.
PH: 713–729–8668
Conversions, sales, service. In business over 15 years.

Electric Vehicle Custom Conversions
1712 Nausika Avenue
Rowland Heights, California 91748
U.S.A.
PH: 818–913–8579
EV conversions, machining services.

Eyeball Engineering
16738 Foothill Boulevard
Fontana, California 92355
U.S.A.
PH: 714–829–2011
Conversion and repair. Recently completed a Honda CRX conversion.

Interesting Transportation, Inc.
2362 Southridge Drive
Palm Springs, California 92264–4960
PH: 619–327–2864
Conversions, research. 30 yrs. experience.

KTA Services
12531 Breezy Way
Orange, California 92669
U.S.A.
PH: 714–639–9799
Proprietor/Engineer – Ken Koch
Proprietor – Judy Koch
Conversions, EV repair and service.

Program Development Associates (of MD)
9140 Centerway Road
Gaithersburg, Maryland 20879
U.S.A.
PH: 301–869–4954
EV Repair & maintenance. Factory–trained to repair Jet EVs and Vehma G–Vans. 15 years hands–on experience with EVs.

San Diego Electric Automobile Company
9011 Los Coches Road
Lakeside, California 92040
U.S.A.
PH: 619–443–3017
Conversion and repair.

Sol Solutions
18422 South Broadway
Gardena, California 90248
U.S.A.
PH: 213–532–4536
FAX: 213–542–6436
President – Robert Hadden
Sales representative for Solar Electric Eng. in Los Angeles area. Conversions, EV repair, demonstations and test drives.

Solar Car Corporation
1300 Lake Washington Road
Melbourne, Florida 32935
U.S.A.
PH: 407–254–2997
FAX: 407–254–4773
Conversion services, kits.

Solar Electric Engineering, Inc.
116 Fourth Street
Santa Rosa, California 95401
U.S.A.
PH: 707–542–1990 FAX: 707–542–4358
Conversion services, kits.

EV DEALERS

Electric Motor Cars
4301 Kingfisher
Houston, Texas 77035
U.S.A
PH: 713-729-8668
Used EV sales & service.

Electric Vehicles, Inc.
2736 Winfield Drive
Mountain View, California 94040
U.S.A.
PH: 415-964-3974
Used EVs.

Jade Mountain
P.O. Box 4616
Boulder, Colorado 80306
U.S.A.
PH: 303-449-6601
FAX: 303-449-8266
New EVs: Zzipper, others.

Kansas Wind Power
Route 1
Holton, Kansas 66436
U.S.A.
PH: 913-364-4407
Mgr. - Bob McBroom
36-volt garden tractors: $750 - 3,000.

Performance Speedway
2810 Algonquin Avenue
Jacksonville, Florida 32210
U.S.A.
New and used EVs, incl. electr. bicycles.

Program Development Associates (of MD)
9140 Centerway Road
Gaithersburg, Maryland 20879
U.S.A.
PH: 301-869-4954
Used EVs from $15,000 to 25,000.

Real Goods Trading Corporation
966 Mazzoni Street
Ukiah, California 95482
U.S.A.
PH: 800-762-7325
FAX: 707-468-0301
New electric motorcycles, Sinclair C5, $1,800 - 2,500.

Sol Solutions
18422 South Broadway
Gardena, California 90248
U.S.A.
PH: 213-532-4536
FAX: 213-542-6436
New and used EVs. Ford Escort: $17,000. Pontiac Fiero: $17,500. Sales rep. for Solar Electric Eng. in Los Angeles area.

Solar Electric Engineering Inc.
116 Fourth Street
Santa Rosa, California 95401
U.S.A.
PH: 707-542-1990
FAX: 707-542-4358
New and used EVs.

Tropico Solar
P.O. Box 417
Big Pine Key, Florida 33043
U.S.A.
PH/FAX: 305-872-3976
Used EVs. Commuta Car: $1,500 to 4,000.

Approximately 250 million gallons of antifreeze were sold in U.S.A. in 1991. It leaks onto roads and is poured down drains, contaminating soil and water. EVs don't use antifreeze.

RENEWABLE ENERGY PRODUCTS

Pollution-free transportation can be achieved by recharging an electric vehicle from sun or wind power. Many individuals who have converted their own standard cars to electric propulsion have fitted a number of photovoltaic (PV) panels on the roofs of the vehicles. Some of these drivers who live in sunny regions have found that such PV panels give them all the recharging capacity they need, because they drive only 30 miles or so per day and keep the vehicle parked in the sun the rest of the day. Most people would probably want greater recharging capacity, requiring more PV panels than could be fit onto the car itself. A photovoltaic recharging system based at home may be a good solution. Windmills or even hydroelectric power might be a better alternative for people in other areas.

The prices for solar and other renewable energy products are slowly coming down again, as the demand increases. Though still initially more expensive than just hooking up to a utility grid, wide spread use of renewable energy can reduce pollution and, of course, dependency on finite fuel reserves such as coal and petroleum.

This is a small listing of some manufacturers, distributors, and retailers of photovoltaic panels and much other equipment related to renewable forms of energy. There is probably at least one retailer of R.E. supplies in every state of the U.S.A. Most of the retailers will also sells their products by mail.

Atlantic Solar Products, Inc.
9351-J Philadelphia Road
P.O. Box 70060
Baltimore, MD 21237
U.S.A.
PH: 301-686-2500
FAX: 301-686-6221
Manager - Bruce Wilson
Retailer of Solarex and Siemens PV panels, various controllers and batteries. A full line catalog is available on request.

B & G Solar
6565 U.S. 41 South
Marquette, Michigan 49855
U.S.A.
PH: 906-249-3935
FAX: 906-249-5177
Retailer of PV panels and other solar equipment.

Bergey Windpower Co.
2001 Priestly Ave.
Norman, Oklahoma 73069
U.S.A.
PH: 405-364-4212
FAX: 405-364-2078
President - Michael Bergey
Mfr. of battery charging wind turbines, 1.5 to 10 kW.

Echo Energy Products
219 Van Ness Avenue
Santa Cruz, California 95060
U.S.A.
PH: 408-423-2429
Gen. Mgr. - George B. Hug
Mfr. of PV powered charging stations, monitor equipment, and high quality PV mounting hardware with tamper-proof highly secure mounts.

Electron Connection
P.O. Box 203
Hornbrook, California 96044
U.S.A.
PH: 916-475-3401
Mfr. and retailer of PVs and controls.

Energy Conservation Services
4110 S.W. 34th Street, Suite 15
Gainesville, Florida 32608
U.S.A.
PH: 904-373-3220
FAX: 904-374-4492
Mfr. of "Solar Power Stations" - complete, tested, and ready-to-use PV charging units. Six different systems, from 1220 to 7300 watt hours per day.

Energy Systems and Design
P.O. Box 1557
Sussex, New Brunswick
CANADA EOE 1PO
CEO - Paul Cunningham
Mfr. and retailer of Micro-Hydro renewable energy products.

Global Light and Power
55 New Montgomery, Suite 424
San Francisco, California 94105
U.S.A.
PH/FAX: 415-495-0494
Retailer of R.E. supplies, with an emphasis on EVs.

Heliotrope General
3733 Kenora Drive
Spring Valley, California 91920
U.S.A.
PH: 619-460-3930
FAX: 619-460-9211
President - Sam Dawson
V.P. - Barry W. Brunye
Administration - Barbara Smith
18 year old mfr. of PV regulators, 120 VAC to 12 VDC battery chargers.

Hoxan America Inc.
One Centennial Plaza
Piscataway, New Jersey 08854
U.S.A.
PH: 908-980-0777
FAX: 908-980-0488
Mfr. of PV modules.

Independent Power & Light
RR 1, Box 3054
Hyde Park, Vermont 05655
U.S.A.
PH: 802-888-7194
Owner - David Palumbo
Retailer of PV modules, batteries, and battery chargers.

Integral Energy Systems
105 Argall Way
Nevada City, California 95959
U.S.A.
PH: 800-735-6790
FAX: 916-265-6151
Retailer of solar and other renewable energy products, books, etc. Catalog: $4

Jade Mountain
P.O. Box 4616
Boulder, Colorado 80306
U.S.A.
PH: 303-449-8266
Mfr. and retailer of PV modules batteries, chargers, DC equipment, motors, books, etc. Catalog available.

Kansas Wind Power
Route 1
Holton, Kansas 66436
U.S.A.
PH: 913-364-4407
Manager - Bob McBroom
Retailer of Todd battery chargers, PV modules, wind generators, etc.

Lake Michigan Wind & Sun
E 3971 Bluebird Road
Forestville, Wisconsin 54213
U.S.A.
PH: 414-837-2267
Mfr. and retailer of wind generators and systems for use with charging EVs.

Photron Inc.
77 West Commercial Street
Willits, California 95490
U.S.A.
PH: 707-459-3211
FAX: 707-459-2165
Sales Mgr. - Vicki Wallace
Sales - Craig Gore
Applications Engr. - Laurence Jennings
Mfr. of PV chargers, controls.

Real Goods Trading Corporation
966 Mazzoni Street
Ukiah, California 95482
U.S.A.
PH: 800-762-7325
PH: 707-468-9214
FAX: 707-468-0301
Retailer of PVs, battery chargers, wind and hydroelectric generators. Has the most complete supply of renewable energy products in the world. Catalog: Free.

Seelye Equipment Specialists (SES)
913 State Street
Charlevoix, Michigan 49720
U.S.A.
PH: 616-547-9430
FAX: 616-547-5522
Wholesaler of flexible PV panels and charge controllers, linear current boosters, etc.

Solar Electric Engineering, Inc.
116 Fourth Street
Santa Rosa, California 95401
U.S.A.
PH: 707-542-1990
FAX: 707-542-4358
Retailer of PVs and other renewable energy products, and a large selection of EVs and related supplies.

Solar Electric Specialties Company
P.O. Box 537
Willits, California 95490
U.S.A.
PH: 707-459-9496
FAX: 707-459-5132
Gen. Mgr. - Paul McClusky
Ind. Sales Mgr. - Scott Williams
Tech. Mgr. - Mike Ashmore
Mfr. of deep cycle lead-acid and gelled-electrolyte batteries for PV systems, optimizer controllers, and packaged solar systems.

Solarex Corporation
1335 Piccard Drive
Rockville, Maryland 20850
U.S.A.
PH: 301-948-0202
FAX: 301-948-7148
A division of Amoco, Solarex mfrs. PV modules and system controllers.

SunAmp Power Company
P.O. Box 6346
Scottsdale, Arizona 85261-6436
U.S.A.
PH: 602-833-1550
FAX: 602-833-1711
President - Lane Garret
Dir. of Marketing - Steve Bass
Wholesale distribution network for custom PV modules, regulators, battery capacity meters, and mounting hardware

Sunelco
100 Skeels Street
P.O. Box 1499
Hamilton, Montana 59840
U.S.A.
Ph: 406-363-6924
800-338-6844 (orders only)
FAX: 406-363-6046
Retailer of R.E. Products, books, etc.

Tropico Solar
P.O. Box 417
Big Pine Key, Florida 33043
U.S.A.
PH: 305-872-3976
FAX: 305-872-3976
Mfr. and retailer of custom-built PV solar systems.

Utility Free
P.O. Box 228
Dept. EVDS
Basalt, Colorado 81621
U.S.A.
PH: 303-927-4568
FAX: 303-927-9421
Sales/Technical - John D'Angelo
Retailer of PV panels, chargers, reconditioned Nickel-Iron and Ni-Cad batteries.

Wind Baron Corporation
3920 E. Huntington
Flagstaff, Arizona 86004
U.S.A.
PH: 602-526-0997
FAX: 602-526-5498
Mfr. of "Windseeker II" wind generator, retailer of PV systems.

World Power Technologies
19 N. Lake Avenue
Duluth, Minnesota 55802
U.S.A.
PH: 218-722-1492
FAX: 218-727-6888
President - Elliott Bayly
Dir. of Marketing - Robert Kohlbry
Mfr. and retailer of wind generators and PV panels.

MISCELLANEOUS EV PARTS & SUPPLIES

Acme Electric Corporation
20 Water Street
Cuba, New York 14727
U.S.A.
Mfr. of battery chargers.

Advanced D.C. Motors, Inc.
219 Lamson Street
Syracuse, New York 13206
U.S.A.
PH: 315-434-9303
FAX: 315-434-9290
Mfr. and supplier of low voltage DC traction and pump motors for EVs and other battery operated equipment.

Baldor Electric
5711 South 7th Street
P.O. Box 244
Fort Smith, Arkansas 72902
PH: 501-646-4711
FAX: 501-648-5792
Mfr. of electric motors suitable for EV propulsion.

Brewer Associates
1310 Sunset Lane
Anacortes, Washington 98221
U.S.A.
PH: 206-293-3201
Mfr. of EV controllers, contactors, thermistors (for measuring battery or motor temperatures), shunts, etc.

Cableform, Inc.
Zion Cross Roads
Troy, Virginia 22974
U.S.A.
PH: 804-589-8224
FAX: 804-589-3803
Mfr. of controllers, contactors, converters.

Curtis Instruments, Inc.
200 Kisco Avenue
Mt. Kisco, New York 10549
U.S.A.
PH: 914-666-2971
Mfr. of electric "fuel" (battery state of charge) gauges, motor controllers, etc. No retail sales, but can provide list of dealers.

Curtis PMC
6591 Sierra Lane
Dublin, California 94568
U.S.A.
PH: 415-828-5001
FAX: 415-833-8777
A division of Curtis Instruments, mfr. of controllers (of speed and torque) of series wound, shunt wound, and permanent magnet motors for EVs.

Dart Controls, Inc.
5000 West 106th Street
P.O. Box 10
Zionsville, Indiana 46077
U.S.A.
Mfr. of motor speed controllers.

Dreisbach ElectroMotive, Inc. (DEMI)
212 Anacapa Street
Santa Barbara, California 93101
U.S.A.
DEMI is developing Zinc-Air batteries for EV propulsion. *No products for sale yet.*

Electric Auto Crafters
2S 643 Nelson Lake Road
Batavia, Illinois 60510
U.S.A.
PH: 708-879-0207 (residence)
Retailer of EV components: motors, controllers, etc.

Electric Vehicles of America, Inc.
P.O. Box 59
Maynard, Massachusetts 01754
U.S.A.
PH: 508-897-9393
FAX: 508-897-1731
President - Robert D. Batson
Retail and mail order sales of EV components: motors, controllers, batteries, chargers, gauges, etc. Catalog: Free.

Electro Automotive
P.O. Box 1113-S
Felton, California 95018-1113
U.S.A.
PH: 408-429-1989
FAX: 408-429-1907
Retail and mail-order sales of EV components: motors, controllers, chargers, gauges, etc. Sells manual for converting an ICE car to electric power ($35). Also offers consultation on conversions. Catalog: $5.

Electronic Transportation Design
P.O. Box 111
Yachats, Oregon 97498
U.S.A.
PH: 503-547-3506
FAX: 503-547-3539
Design Engineer - Clarence W. Ellers
Retailer of controllers, batteries, and special EV products. Locator specialist.

Eyeball Engineering
16738 Foothill Boulevard
Fontana, California 92355
U.S.A.
PH: 714-829-2011
Sells misc. EV parts: motors, adapter plates, etc. Does EV conversions.

General Electric Company
6801 Industrial Drive
P.O. Box 489
Mebane, North Carolina 27302
U.S.A.
PH: 919-563-7537
FAX: 919-563-7301
Mgr., sales & Mktg. - Glenn Nalls
Sales Engineer - Rick Hauser
Mfr. of EV traction motors, controllers, and other equipment.

Global Light and Power
55 New Montgomery, Suite 424
San Francisco, California 94105
U.S.A.
PH/FAX: 415-495-0494
Int'l. trading co. specializing in R.E. technology. Operates education and technology transfer programs, offers business assistance for those interested in R.E.

J.C. Whitney & Company
1917-19 Archer Avenue
P.O. Box 8410
Chicago, Illinois 60680
U.S.A.
PH: 312-431-6102
FAX: 312-431-6199
Large mail-order supplier of automotive & cycle parts, supplies, equip. Catalog: $1.

Johnson Controls
900 Keefe Avenue
Milwaukee, Wisconsin 53212
U.S.A.
PH: 800-365-777
FAX: 414-961-6506
Mfr. of batteries, controls, and other equipment for EVs.

Kaylor-Kit
P.O. Box 9400
Stanford, California 94305
U.S.A.
PH: 415-325-6900
EV conversion kits.

KTA Services
12531 Breezy Way
Orange, California 92669
U.S.A.
PH: 714-639-9799
Proprieter, Engr. - Ken Koch
Proprieter - Judy Koch
Retailer of motors, controllers, etc.

Lester Electrical
625 West A Street
Lincoln, Nebraska 68522
U.S.A.
PH: 402-477-8988
FAX: 402-474-1769
Mfr. of battery chargers and other electrical components.

Livos Plant Chemistry
1365 Rufina Circle
Santa Fe, New Mexico 87501
U.S.A.
PH: 505-438-3448
Mfr. & supplier of paints, varnishes, nonstructural adhesives, etc. made entirely from plant materials. May be of use in auto interiors, rather than using petrochemicals.

Prestolite Electric, Inc.
4 SeaGate
Toledo, Ohio 43691-0904
U.S.A.
PH: 419-249-7600
FAX: 419-249-7637
V.P. Mktg./Industrial sales – T.R. Jennett
Mfr. of electric propulsion motors up to about 30 hp, suitable for EVs. Does not sell to individuals but can give specifications and a list of distributors.

Rexnord Corporation
Stearns Division
120 North Broadway
Milwaukee, Wisconsin 53202
U.S.A.
PH: 414-272-1100
Mfr. of capacitors, switches, electrically set clutches and brakes, and other items, some applicable to EVs.

Ross Engineering Corporation
540 Westchester Drive
Campbell, California 95008
U.S.A.
PH: 408-377-4621
FAX: 408-377-5182
Mfr. of high voltage relays, three-phase vacuum contactors, and circuit breakers.

San Diego Electric Automobile Company
9011 Los Coches Road
Lakeside, California 92040
U.S.A.
PH: 619-443-3017
Retailer of EV conversion kits.

Sevcon, Inc.
40 North Avenue
Burlington, Massachusetts 01830
U.S.A.
PH: 617-272-3612
FAX: 617-272-1953
Established in the U.K. in 1961, Sevcon is a leading mfr. of electronic motor control equipment for EVs. Products include: Controllers, converters, accelerators, etc.

Solar Car Corporation
1300 Lake Washington Road
Melbourne, Florida 32935
U.S.A.
PH: 407-254-2997
FAX: 407-254-4773
EV components, conversion kits.
Catalog: $5.

Solar Electric Engineering, Inc.
116 Fourth Street
Santa Rosa, California 95401
U.S.A.
PH: 707-542-1990
FAX: 707-542-4358
Retailer of EV components: motors, controllers, etc. and EV conversion kits.

Solectria Corporation
27 Jason Street
Arlington, Massachusetts 02174
U.S.A.
PH: 617-894-6670
FAX: 617-894-9522
CEO/Dir. R & D – James Worden
President – Anita Rajan
Mfr. & supplier of EV propulsion motors (AC & DC), controllers, and other components. Also developing new EVs and conversions.

Soleq Corporation
5969 North Elston Avenue
Chicago, Illinois 60646
U.S.A.
PH: 312-792-3811
FAX 312-792-0315
312-792-2164
Developer and mfr. of controllers, chargers, converters, and other EV components. Definitely not interested in selling to individuals or kit builders.

TAP Plastics Inc.
6475 Sierra Lane
Dublin, California 94568
U.S.A.
PH: 415-829-4889
FAX: 415-829-6921
Mfr. of acrylic plastic sheets, lettering, forms, fiberglass materials, specialty paints, etc. Catalog: Free.

Trace Engineering
5916 195th NE
Arlington, Washington 98223
U.S.A.
PH: 206-435-8826
FAX: 206-435-2229
Mktg. Dir. - Bob Summers
Mfr. of power inverters.

Twenty First Century Electric Vehicles
8136 Byron Road
Suite G
Whittier, California 90606
U.S.A.
PH: 213-593-8612
Former mfr. of EVs. Now services some EV components. Also doing research into future transportation possibilities in which electric motors are installed in roads to propel vehicles.

Unique Mobility, Inc.
3700 South Jason Street
Englewood, Colorado 80110
U.S.A.
PH: 303-761-2137
FAX: 303-761-3218
Mfr. and supplier of EV traction motors and controllers. Many of the top competing solar cars use Unique's motors.

Westberg Manufacturing, Inc.
3400 Westach Way
Sonoma, California 95476
U.S.A.
PH: 707-938-2121
FAX: 707-938-4968
V.P. Des. - G. L. Westberg
V.P. Admin. - R. R. Westberg
Mfr. of voltage, amperage, battery and motor temp. gauges for EVs.

WirthCo Engineering, Inc.
8131 Pennsylvania Circle, Suite 100
Bloomington, Minnesota 55438
U.S.A.
PH: 612-941-9073
FAX: 612-941-0659
President - Steven E. Wirth
Mfr. of battery quick disconnect switches.

SOLAR CAR CORPORATION
Electric Vehicles and Components
Look No More!
Everything You Need For Your Conversion
State Of The Art Components
Send $5.00 for our New Catalog
Refundable with order. Allow 6 weeks for delivery.
NAME ____________
ADDRESS ____________
CITY ____________ STATE ____ ZIP ______
Mail To: *SOLAR CAR CORPORATION*
1300 Lake Washington Rd.•Melbourne, FL 32935

EURASIA

Jürg Tschepen
JT Design
Flurystrasse 9
8620 Wetzikon
SWITERLAND
PH: 932 15 51
FAX: 01 932 43 70

Calypso Electric

The Calypso Electric LEV (Light-Electro-Vehicle) is the latest design by Jürg Tschepen. He built two predecessors, Calypso P1 and P2, which also featured composite construction. The Calypso Electric is designed solely for electric propulsion and seats two to four people. The two rear seats fold, thus providing a variable loading area. This car has two side doors and a large, top-hinged rear door that reaches right down to the floor, allowing easy access for loading. Construction is of aluminum, steel, honeycomb sheets, and other materials. The prototype has energy-absorbing composite cells for additional safety in the event of an impact. Twelve 12-volt batteries are used, providing a total of 144 volts in the system. The standard suspension and axles from the Citroen AX are used; these are more than adequate for the Calypso Electric, which weighs less. Front wheel drive is used, powered by an asynchronous electric motor. The price of the vehicle will depend on the quantity produced.

Seats	4
Length	3.20 m (10 ft 6 in)
Height	1.39 m (4 ft 7 in)
Width	1.55 m (5 ft 1 in)
Wheelbase	2.02 m (6 ft 7½ in)
Empty Weight (incl. twelve 90Ah batteries)	770 kg (1,697 lbs)
Motor	Biral 12 kW (16 hp)
Top Speed	85 kph (53 mph)
Range	120 km (75 miles)

S.E.E.R.- Volta
(Societe Europeenne Des Electromobiles Rochelaises)
Avenue Paul Langevin
B.P. 6
17182 Perigny Cedex
FRANCE
PH: 011-33-46-45-25-05
FAX: 011-33-46-44-71-62
General Manager - Jack Vergne
Chairman and Managing Director - Bernard Long
Commercial Attache - Florence Gaudin

VOLTA

S.E.E.R. manufactures three versions of the electric VOLTA utility vehicle. The battery pack consists of 16 sealed lead-acid batteries manufactured by Oldham, and weighs 480 kilograms. The vehicle has regenerative braking as standard equipment. Rear side windows are available as an option on the van. The vehicle frame is made of metal, and the body of tinted polyester. A manual Peugeot four-speed transmission is used. The price for the van is 158,000 FF, the pick-up is 163,000 FF, and the platform vehicle sells for 154,000 FF.

Seats	2
Length	3.25 m (10 ft 7½ in)
Height	1.77 m (5 ft 10 in)
Width	1.56 m (5 ft 1½ in)
Wheelbase	1.74 m (5 ft 8½ in)
Empty Weight	1,220 kg (2,689 lbs)
Gross Weight	1,700 kg (3,747 lbs)
Motor	11 kW (15 hp)
Top Speed	73 kph (45 mph)
Consumption	20 to 25 kW per 100 km
Range	80 km (50 miles)

ASSOCIATIONS

Association Europeenne Des Vehicules Electriques Routiers
Boulevard de Waterloo, 34
100 Bruxelles, BELGIUM
European EV ass'n.

Battery and Solar Vehicle Society
44 Heath Road
Market Bosworth
Nuneaton, Warwicks CV13 ONX
ENGLAND, U.K.
Ass'n. to promote development and use of EVs. Publishes bimonthly *"Battery Vehicle Review"*.

Electric Vehicle Association
8 Leicester Street
London, WC2H 7BN
ENGLAND, U.K.
PH: (44) 071 872 6205
FAX: (44) 071 734 2354
Trade assn. of mfrs. of electric industrial and road vehicles, batteries, and components. Published 150 page manual on EV operating procedures.

International Electric Vehicle Symposium
Symposium Secretariat, EVS-11
c/o CEI-CIVES
Viale Monza 259
I-20126 Milano
ITALIA
PH: 39.2.257731
FAX: 39.2.25773210
The electric vehicle symposium is held in a different country each year. This year (1992), is the 11th symposium and it is to be held in Italy.

Registro Italiano Veicoli Elettro Solari (RIVES)
Sede Legale: Via Unione 3-20122 Milano
ITALIA
FAX: 0039/2/39322954
Ass'n. for the study and promotion of EVs, and to exchange information between Italian and foreign clubs/associations.

BATTERIES

Chloride Industrial Batteries Group
P.O. Box 5
Clifton Junction
Swinton
Manchester M27 2LR
ENGLAND, U.K.
Mfr. of lead-acid batteries suitable for EV propulsion.

Electrona Ltd. (SA)
CH-2017 Boudry
SWITZERLAND
PH: 038 44 2121
FAX: 038 42 1517
Mfr. of batteries, chargers, and other equipment for EVs.

Oldham Crompton Batteries Ltd.
Edward Street, Denton
Denton, Manchester M34 3AT
ENGLAND, U.K.
PH: 061 335 0999
FAX: 061 335 0020
European Mktg. Mgr. - Johme Raham
Large mfr. of batteries suitable for EVs.

MISCELLANEOUS EV PARTS & SUPPLIES

City-Com A/S
Haraldsvej 66
DK-8900 Randers
DENMARK
Following a recent name change, City-Com is still presumably marketing the Mini-El single seat lightweight EV. About 4,000 of these vehicles have been sold, but we have no recent news from them.

Curtis Instruments GmbH
Senefelder Strasse 7A
4790 Paderborn, GERMANY
PH: 49 (05251) 5 50 26
FAX: 49 (05251) 54 11 30
Mfr. of various electrical components.

Curtis Instruments S.A.
98 Bld. Victor Hugo
92110 Clichy
FRANCE
PH: 33(1) 47 31 6110
FAX: 33(1) 42 70 3426
General Manager - Martine Petrelluzzi
Tech. Manager - Jacques Legros
Product Manager - Jean Luc. Gautier
Mfr. of speed controllers, battery discharge indicators, hour meters.

Curtis Instruments (UK) Ltd.
51 Grafton Street
Northampton, NN1 2NT
ENGLAND, U.K.
PH: 44 (0604) 29755
FAX: 44 (0604) 29876
Mfr. of various electrical components.

Electric Vehicle Systems
10 Donkin Road
Armstrong Industrial Estate
Washington, Tyne & Wear NE37 1PF
U.K.
PH: 091 417 8811
FAX: 091 415 4219
Director - Ken Greaves
Mfr. of battery chargers, control systems, power supplies, and EV accessories.

Electricars
O.E. Production Plant
Unit 15
Carlyon Road Industrial Estate
Atherstone, Warwickshire CV9 1LQ
ENGLAND, U.K.
PH: 0827 716888
FAX: 0827 717841
Mfr. of ready-to-drive electric utility vehicles, incl. street-legal delivery trucks. Speeds to 35 kph (22 mph). No passenger vehicles available.

Sevcon Ltd.
Kingsway
Gateshead NE 11 0QA
ENGLAND, U.K.
PH: 091-487-8516
FAX: 091-482-4223
Established in 1961, Sevcon is a leading mfr. of electronic motor control equipment for EVs.

Sevcon SA
12 Rue Jean Poulmarch
95100 Argenteuil
FRANCE
PH: 134-109-9545
FAX: 134-106-6138
Mfr. of controllers, converters, accelerators, etc.

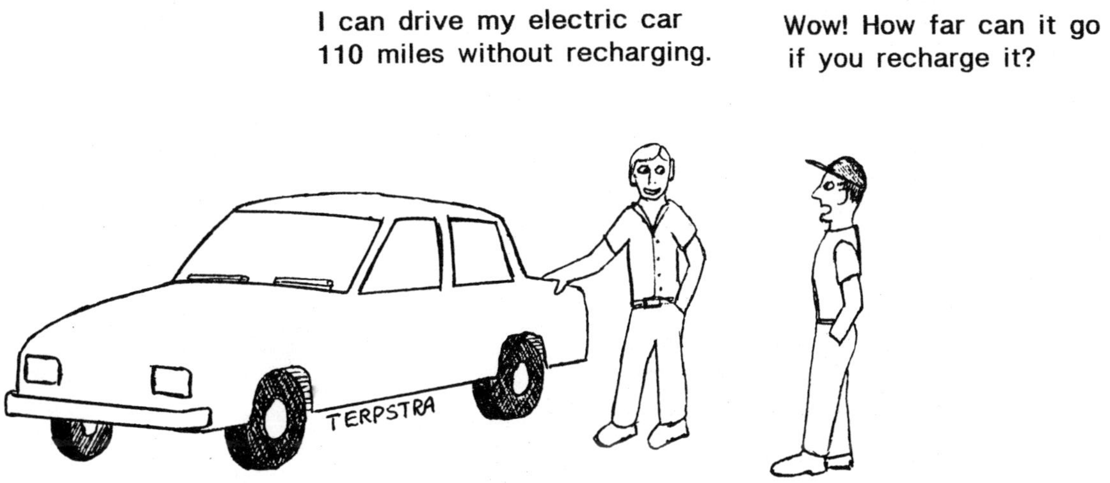

So tell me — How do you get such excellent range?
My electric car goes only 20 miles between charges.
Have you got some special high–tech batteries?

PACIFIC

Elroy Engineering Pty. Ltd.
20 Lutanda Close
Pennant Hills, New South Wales 2120
AUSTRALIA
PH: 02 481 9385
FAX: 02 980 7021

Elroy Engineering has invested 22 years in research, development, prototyping, and testing of purpose-built electric cars, vans, trucks, and buses. Third-generation TOWNOBILES from 5 to 300 passenger or ¼ to 20 ton capacity, are now developed and ready for volume production, in regions where effective after sales service can be provided. All models are also available for prior sales at this time. The TOWNOBILE vehicles utilize lightweight yet rugged monocoque construction and feature "Motor-in-Wheels" drive units. The dual front wheels rotate around a central electric motor. (Larger TOWNOBILE models have a slightly different arrangement.) These and other features allow the TOWNOBILE electric vehicles to be lighter than ICE powered vehicles of similar capacity.

A typical TOWNOBILE model is the B10B Electric Multi-Purpose Vehicle illustrated below. 0ther models are B5B, B15B, B20, B25 MPVs and B70, B90, B120, B140, B180, B220, B250, B280, and B300 Single, Double-Deck, Wide-Body and Articulated buses in Battery, Trolley, and Trolley-Battery variants. For more specific and up-to-date information, contact Elroy Engineering at the address above.

ELROY 'TOWNOBILE'® B10B PRODUCTION MODEL

	TOWNOBILE B10B Multi-Purpose EV	B15B Van, Mini-Bus
Seats	5–10	10–15
Length	3.90 m (12 ft 9 in)	4.475 m (14 ft 10 in)
Height	1.60 m (5 ft 3 in)	1.80 m (5 ft 11 in)
Width	1.90 m (6 ft 3 in)	1.90 m (6 ft 3 in)
Curb Weight	1500 kg (3306 lbs)	1700 kg (3747 lbs)
Gross Weight	2100 kg (4628 lbs)	2600 kg (5730 lbs)
Wheelbase	2.80 m (9 ft 2 in)	3.40 m (11 ft 2 in)
Top Speed	88 kph (55 mph)	88 kph (55 mph)
Acceleration, 0–60 kph	13 seconds	13 seconds
Range, city	80 km (50 miles)	80 km (50 miles)

L & J Huntington Enterprises Pty. Ltd.
2 Broos Road
Oakville, New South Wales 2765
AUSTRALIA
045-877-371

Mira ECC

The Mira ECC (Electric Commuter Car) is the first commercially available electric car in Australia. A new EV conversion, this car is imported from Japan and then equipped with suitable electric propulsion components at the L & J Huntington facilities in Sydney. The Mira ECC is intended primarily for urban use in commuting and shopping errands. The battery pack can be recharged from a standard 240-volt power outlet and has about a 600 charge cycle life. (This should last three to four years.) Contact the company at the address above for pricing and other information. The specifications for this vehicle are shown below. Designer Les Puklowski has additional vehicles planned for future availability, including a four-place petrol-electric hybrid vehicle.

Seats	2
Length	3.295 m (10 ft 9½ in)
Height	1.415 m (4 ft 7½ in)
Wheelbase	2.280 m (7 ft 6 in)
Turning Circle	4.5 m (14 ft 9 in)
Curb Weight	770 kg (1,697 lbs)
Gross Weight	1,040 kg (2,295 lbs)
Motor	7 kW (9.4 hp)
Controller	Curtis PMC
Transmission	4 speed manual gearbox
Maximum Speed	85 kph (53 mph)
Range	50 - 80 km (31 - 50 miles)

ASSOCIATIONS

Australian Electric Vehicle Association Inc.
P.O. Box 273
Mitcham, Victoria
AUSTRALIA
PH: 61-3722 1416
FAX: 61-3722 2028
President - John Stevens
Secretary - John Hill
EV association. Annual dues, $30 (add $10 for air mail), includes monthly newsletter "Electric Vehicle News".

Energy Promotions
1074 Pacific Highway
Pymble, New South Wales 2073
AUSTRALIA
PH: 61-2-9884255
FAX: 61-2-4498767
Manager - H. Tholstrup
Association that organizes EV events and publishes newsletters and reports.

Japan Electric Vehicle Association
Sakura Building 2-5-5
Toranomon Minato-ku
Tokyo, JAPAN
Trade association of Japanese auto manufacturers developing EVs.

New Zealand Electric Car Owners Club
26 Victoria Road
Papatoetoe, Auckland
NEW ZEALAND
PH: 277 5462
FAX: 277 6412
New Zealand's largest specialist car club, has over 1,000 members.

BOOKS

Office of Energy
Department of Mineral Resources
P.O. Box 536
St. Leonards, New South Wales 2065
AUSTRALIA
PH: 02-901-8269
FAX: 02-901-8247
Publisher and retailer of *Solar and Electric Vehicles* and many titles on renewable energy. Also publishes various reports and the *Energy Focus* newsletter.

COMPOSITE FRP MATERIALS

Universal Plastics
P.O. Box 76
Cloverdale, WA 6105
AUSTRALIA
PH: 09-361-8316
FAX: 09-277-3718
Retailer of fiberglass and other materials.

RENEWABLE ENERGY

Solarex Corporation
18th Floor, Sincere Insurance Building
4 Hennessey Road
HONG KONG
PH: 852-528-5717
FAX: 852-527-9704

Solarex Pty. Ltd.
78 Biloela Street Villawood
P.O. Box 204
Chester Hill, New South Wales 2163
AUSTRALIA
PH: 61-2-7274455
FAX: 61-2-7277447

MISCELLANEOUS

Vossloh Schwabe Australia Pty. Ltd.
24 Hudson Street
Castle Hill, New South Wales 2154
AUSTRALIA
PH: (02) 680-5800
FAX: (02) 680-5888
Nat'l. Sales Mgr. - John Toyer
Mfr. of transformers to 5KVA and battery chargers up to 250 amps.

SAY YOU SAW IT IN THE *EVD*

GLOSSARY

AC	Alternating Current
CNG	Compressed Natural Gas
DC	Direct Current
DOE	Department of Energy
EHP	Electric and Hybrid Propulsion
EV	Electric Vehicle
ICE	Internal Combustion Engine
kW	Kilowatt(s)
kWh	Kilowatt-hour(s)
LNG	Liquified Natural Gas
OTT	Office of Transportation Technologies
PV	Photovoltaic (solar) cells or panels
RE	Renewable Energy
SASE	Self-Addressed, Stamped Envelope
SLI	Starting-Lighting-Ignition; the type of battery used in conventional vehicles
SMOG	A mixture of SMoke and fOG. This term is often used erroneously to refer to air pollution in general. Denver and Phoenix, though highly polluted, seldom have smog.
SOC	State Of Charge
ZEV	Zero Emission Vehicle

INDEX

DON'T REPLACE YOUR CAR,

RECYCLE IT!

Convert From Gas To Electricity

GET INFO & COMPONENTS FROM THE ELECTRIC CAR EXPERTS SINCE 1979.

****$5.00 for catalog of components & kits, all manufacturer new.***

****37.50 for CONVERT IT, a step-by-step illustrated how-to manual.***

INTRODUCING THE

VOLTSRABBIT™

A complete bolt-in kit for converting a gas or diesel Rabbit to electricity. No design or fabrication needed! Full conversion can be done in one week.

SAVE MONEY:

*Operating costs for an electric car are only 1/3 of costs for a gas car.

SAVE TIME:

*Electric cars mean low maintenance and high reliability, so they spend a lot less time at the repair shop.

SAVE THE PLANET:

*Electric cars produce no emissions.
*Electric cars use no coolant or oil.
*A gas car "recycled" to electricity is on the road--not in a landfill.

ELECTRO AUTOMOTIVE
THE SYMBOL OF EXCELLENCE
IN ELECTRIC VEHICLES

P. O. BOX 1113-S FELTON, CA 95018-1113 (408) 429-1989

WE WROTE THE BOOK.

RAINFORESTS

YOU CAN LIVE WITH THEM

Rainforest being cleared in Central America for growing citrus.

More than half the species of plants and animals on earth live in tropical rainforests. About 1,500 species of birds are indigenous to the rainforests of Indonesia. The island of Borneo has approximately 3,000 species of trees, compared to about 865 species in North America, and fewer than 40 in the entire British isles. Rainforests (temperate as well as tropical) are absolutely essential to maintaining climatic stability. But they are being destroyed at an alarming rate. In the wake of this annihilation, weather patterns are disrupted, causing severe droughts in some areas and floods in others. Topsoil is lost, washed into the sea. Many forest plant an animal species live in symbiotic relationships. When one is wiped out, more are lost as a direct consequence. About 17,000 species are lost each year because of rainforest destruction. Hundreds of indigenous people groups also depend directly on the rainforests for their livelihood.

What can be done to halt the devastation? The unchecked greed of many large corporations is a big factor, but we must also examine our own lifestyles and see what changes we can make to slow the damage. One big positive step is to give up eating beef. The cattle connection is perhaps the second greatest single cause of rainforest destruction. (The first, of course, is human overpopulation.) Millions of acres of rainforest are destroyed to make pasture land for cattle, to supply North America and other markets with beef. This industry also hurts the poor people in those countries; they are economically forced off of their land to make way for big agribusinesses. Not only tropical regions are adversely affected by the beef industry. About half the the land in the U.S.A. is used in some way (grazing, growing feed grain, etc.) for raising cattle.

Drink less orange juice. Citrus drinks are healthy products, and having some groves worldwide doesn't pose a major threat. But when huge tracts of virgin rainforest are cleared to grow oranges, this has serious consequences. The massive amount of vegetation lost by clearing the forest is not replaced by planting a relatively open orange grove. And again, the great biotic diversity of plant and animal species is lost. The opportunities that these species might have had to improve the quality of life for human beings (thru food, medicine, and other products) cannot be known.

We Need Your Help

I hope you have found the ***Electric Vehicle Directory*** useful in learning about the electric cars that are available today. Perhaps you will find one of the vehicles listed here to be suitable for your transportation needs.

We would like to update this publication annually and desire your help to ensure that future editions are as complete, accurate, and up-to-date as possible. Do you know of an electric car design that is commercially available (ready-to-drive, or in the form of plans or kits) that is not listed here? Are you aware of manufacturers or suppliers of electric vehicle components that are not listed here but should be? Please inform me. Thank you for your help.

Philip Terpstra, Author/Compiler

IS THIS YOUR OWN COPY?

Did you borrow this copy of the ***Electric Vehicle Directory*** from a library or a friend? Wouldn't you rather have your own copy for quick, handy reference? Fill out your name and address below, or use a separate sheet of paper, and order your own copy today!

1992 Electric Vehicle Directory prices:
(In U.S. dollars)
In U.S.A. - $11 postpaid
Canada - $12 postpaid
Elsewhere - $15 postpaid, by air

Send a check or money order, drawn on a U.S. bank (with proper bank routing numbers on the bottom of the check) to:

SPIRIT PUBLICATIONS
P.O. Box 23417
Tucson, Arizona 85734
U.S.A.

Name and Address: ______________________________

____

____

____

No. of Copies Ordered:__________ **Total Enclosed:**______________